616.4
SIL
Silverstein, Robert
 Diabetes

	DATE DUE		

—Diseases and People—

DIABETES

Alvin, Virginia, and Robert
Silverstein

Enslow Publishers, Inc.
40 Industrial Road   PO Box 38
Box 398   Aldershot
Berkeley Heights, NJ 07922   Hants GU12 6BP
USA   UK
http://www.enslow.com

For John and Joan Nunn

Library of Congress Cataloging-in-Publication Data

Silverstein, Alvin.
  Diabetes / Alvin, Virginia, and Robert Silverstein.
    p. cm.—(Diseases and people)
  Includes bibliographical references and index.
  ISBN 0-89490-464-7
    1. Diabetes—Juvenile literature. I. Silverstein, Virginia B.
II. Silverstein, Robert A. III. Title. IV. Series.
RC660.5.S55   1994
616.4'62—dc20   93-41199
                                                           CIP
                                                            AC

Printed in the United States of America

10 9 8 7 6

To Our Readers:
All Internet Addresses in this book were active and appropriate when we went to press. Any
comments or suggestions can be sent by e-mail to Comments@enslow.com or to the address
on the back cover.

Illustration Credits: The Bettmann Archive, Inc., pp. 15, 17; Centers for Disease
Control, p. 43; Eli Lilly and Company, p. 19; ©Erik Hansen 1992 / Medisense,
Inc., p 73; The Jackson Laboratory, p. 91; Novo Nordisk Pharmaceuticals, Inc.,
p. 61; Patrick Dyson, Health Science Center, University of Florida, pp. 53, 86, 89;
People Weekly © 1993 Steve Schapiro, p. 77; ©1993 Sue Owrutsky, pp. 64, 75;
UPI/Bettmann, p. 32.

Cover Illustration: SPL / Custom Medical Stock Photo

Contents

Acknowledgments

The authors would like to thank Dr. Patrick Dyson of the University of Florida, Martha M. Funnell of the University of Michigan Medical Center, Dr. Paul E. Lacy of the Washington University School of Medicine in St. Louis, the American Diabetes Association, the Canadian Diabetes Association, the Joslin Diabetes Center, the Juvenile Diabetes Foundation, Lifescan Inc., MediSense Inc., the National Diabetes Information Clearinghouse, Novo Nordisk Pharmaceuticals, Inc., Sandia National Laboratories, and all the others who so kindly provided information and photographs for this book.

Also thanks to Dr. Harold Starkman of the Columbia University College of Physicians and Surgeons, for his careful reading of the text and his many helpful comments and suggestions.

TYPE I DIABETES

What is it? A disease in which the body is unable to effectively store and use glucose as an energy source.

Also called insulin-dependent diabetes mellitus (IDDM) because the beta cells of the pancreas do not produce enough insulin.

Who gets it? Both sexes; mainly children, teens, and young adults; rare among Asians, Africans, and Native Americans.

How do you get it? Partly hereditary; appears to be triggered by a virus infection.

What are the symptoms? Urgent thirst, excessive urination, weight loss, fatigue, irritability.

Uncontrolled diabetes can lead to complications including retinopathy and blindness, kidney disease, and heart disease.

How is it treated? Insulin injections; diet and exercise.

How can it be prevented? Low-dose insulin or immunosuppressives in early stages (still experimental).

TYPE II DIABETES

What is it? A disease in which the body is unable to effectively store and use glucose as an energy source.

Also called non-insulin-dependent diabetes mellitus (NIDDM) because insulin may be produced but is ineffective.

Who gets it? Mainly obese middle-aged and old people; nearly all races.

How do you get it? Hereditary; triggered by obesity.

What are the symptoms? Urgent thirst, excessive urination, weight loss, fatigue, irritability; also frequent infections, blurred vision, slow healing, tingling or numbness. Uncontrolled diabetes can lead to complications including retinopathy and blindness, kidney disease, and heart disease.

How is it treated? Diet and exercise; oral hypoglycemic drugs or insulin may also be needed.

How can it be prevented? Diet, exercise, and other weight-loss measures.

The Sugar Disease

1

At nineteen, Dionne was leading a busy, happy life. She was living on her own for the first time, attending college, working part-time in a chiropractor's office to earn part of her expenses, and enjoying parties and dates.

A routine urine test when she went to the doctor changed Dionne's life forever. The test showed the presence of sugar—something that is not normally found in urine. A nurse pricked Dionne's fingertip with a sharp lancet and tested the drop of blood that welled out. "Borderline," she said, shaking her head. "Maybe we should schedule some more tests."

The follow-up tests told an upsetting story. There was a little more than the normal amount of sugar in Dionne's blood. After she drank a cup of sugary liquid there was a sharp rise; sugar had passed from Dionne's stomach into her bloodstream. That was perfectly normal. But the later test results were not. A healthy person's body quickly stores sugar away after a meal, but in Dionne's case most of the sugar was still in her blood, even after three hours.

"You have diabetes," the doctor said and then explained some of what that diagnosis meant. This wasn't something like a cold or some other illness that makes you miserable for a while and then goes away. Dionne would have diabetes all her life. And she would have to change her life-style, keeping to a careful diet, testing her blood sugar level, and giving herself injections of insulin.

At a diabetes center Dionne was trained in all the routines of caring for herself, and she learned to apply them to her daily life. She takes insulin shots twice a day now, morning and evening, and she carefully watches her diet—at least, most of the time. "There are so many temptations," she sighs. "Sometimes I splurge"—like the time she absent-mindedly snacked on raisins while she was cooking Thanksgiving dinner for her family—"and then I feel totally wiped out for two days." Her busy life doesn't always allow her to be as regular as she should be; it's difficult to fit in her evening insulin shot at the right time if she is out with friends, and sometimes she forgets to eat on schedule. But, in general, her diabetes is fairly well controlled, and her friends have been understanding about her special routines. "It's no big deal," she says. "Actually, practically everybody is on some kind of diet of their own."[1]

The "Sugar Disease"

In diabetes, which is sometimes called the "sugar disease," the body either does not produce or doesn't properly use insulin, a hormone that helps the body to get needed energy from sugar. Scientists have learned that diabetes actually is not a single disease. There are two main types. In Type I diabetes, which affects mainly children, teens, and young adults, the pancreas produces little or no insulin. From 90 to 95 percent of adults with diabetes have Type II, which develops most commonly in middle-aged and elderly people. In Type II diabetes, the body may be producing insulin, but it is unable to use the hormone effectively.

In both types of diabetes, the body can't handle sugar properly; it accumulates in the blood, and excess sugar may spill over into the urine. When diabetes is uncontrolled, serious complications may develop, including high blood pressure, kidney failure, blindness, and nerve damage.

At least 100 million people in the world have diabetes.[2] This disease has been diagnosed in nearly seven million Americans, and medical specialists suspect that another seven million may have diabetes without knowing it.[3] In addition to personal suffering, diabetes costs society over $40 billion each year in health care expenses, disability payments, and lost earnings.[4]

Despite these statistics, we have means of treating the disease that permit many people with diabetes to live full, normal lives. Some exciting research now going on promises to reveal much more in the future. Many are hopeful that soon we may have a cure for this widespread disease.

2
Diabetes Through the Ages

The oldest written reference to diabetes is found in the Ebers papyrus, which was written in ancient Egypt about 1500 B.C. The Egyptian physicians suggested treatments for *polyuria* (frequent urination—one of the most obvious signs of diabetes) that included eating wheat grains, grapes, honey, and berries.

The ancient Greek physician Aretaeus of Cappadocia gave diabetes its name, which is the Greek word for "siphon." About A.D.100 he described the disease as "a melting down of the flesh and limbs into urine." Diabetes was rare in his time, and for its sufferers, he wrote, "Life is short, disgusting, and painful."[1] Listing such symptoms as burning thirst and incessant urination, he suggested a diet of milk, gruel, cereal, and wine.

Diabetes was also well known to medical specialists in

ancient China, Japan and India. For example, Susruta, a doctor in India around 400 B.C., wrote about a disease in which people produced "honey urine," "like an elephant's in quantity."[2] He noted that the urine of a person with diabetes attracts flies. Other ancient Indian writers described such symptoms as thirst, fatigue, and skin boils. They reported that diabetes is a disease most often found among the rich and self-indulgent, who are fond of eating to excess; they also suggested that the disease might be hereditary. But they had no cures to offer.

In the West, Roman physicians added the Latin word *mellitus* (meaning "sweet" or "honeyed") to the name of the disease. But then came the Dark Ages, when much of the old knowledge was lost.

Rediscovering Diabetes

During the Renaissance, doctors began laboriously rediscovering some of the ancient knowledge. The sixteenth-century Swiss physician Paracelsus, for example, found a white powder when he evaporated the urine of a person with diabetes, but mistakenly thought it was salt. In 1683 another Swiss physician, Johann Conrad Brunner, removed the pancreases of dogs and found that they suffered from great thirst and excessive urination, but he did not realize that he had created an experimental model of diabetes.

In 1766 an English physician, Matthew Dobson, made the first new breakthrough. He proved chemically that the sweetness of the urine was due to the presence of sugar. He also found sugar in the blood of both healthy people and those with diabetes, and he suggested that the sugar in the urine of people with diabetes came from their blood.

Doctors had to taste their patients' urine to determine whether sugar was present until the early nineteenth century, when German physician Johann Frank invented a yeast test for sugar. Around this time, doctors such as British physician John Rollo were experimenting with low-carbohydrate diets in the treatment of diabetes, and during the 1800s a high fat intake, green vegetables, and exercise typically were prescribed. Such treatments sometimes helped people with diabetes get better—especially if they were obese older people. But there was little that doctors could do for children with diabetes, and they usually had only a few months to live.

The doctors did not know what caused diabetes. Eighteenth-century English physician Thomas Cawley, who was the first to diagnose diabetes on the basis of sugar in the urine, had thought it was a kidney disease.

In 1889 European medical researchers Joseph von Mering and Oskar Minkowski were trying to prove that the pancreas is involved in the digestion of fats. They removed the pancreas of a dog to see what would happen. After the operation the dog began to urinate uncontrollably, as Brunner's dogs had more than two hundred years earlier. Von Mering and Minkowski found that the dog's urine contained sugar; it had developed diabetes. Unlike Brunner, they concluded that diabetes was a disease of the pancreas. But the pancreas is a digestive gland, producing substances to help break down food. What could it have to do with diabetes?

Zeroing in on the Pancreas

Another piece of the puzzle was already in place, waiting to be recognized. In 1869 a brilliant German medical student, Paul Langerhans, had noticed clusters of cells (now called islets of Langerhans) scattered throughout the pancreas. Other researchers followed up his work and discovered that the islets have nothing to do with the digestive functions of the pancreas but instead are endocrine glands, whose job is to produce hormones. Autopsies of people with diabetes, performed in 1902 at Johns Hopkins University in Baltimore, revealed that their islets of Langerhans had degenerated. Laboratory studies helped to confirm the link between the islets and diabetes. In experiments on animals, the ducts of the pancreas were tied off; the gland shriveled, but the islets of Langerhans remained undamaged, and no symptoms of diabetes appeared. But if the whole pancreas was removed, or if the islets were damaged, diabetes developed.

Meanwhile, two different types of islet cells, alpha and beta cells, were identified, and scientists theorized that each produced a hormone. In the early 1900s, several researchers suggested that one of the pancreatic hormones controlled the body's use of sugar, and proposed that it be called insulin, after the Latin word *insula*, meaning "island." But efforts to isolate the hormone were frustrating, and extracts of the pancreas proved quite ineffective in treating diabetes.

The Hunt for the Hormone

Soon after the end of World War I, a young Canadian ortho-pedic surgeon named Frederick Banting read about the experiments in which the ducts of the pancreas were tied off. He was particularly interested in diabetes because a neighbor's child had recently died of the disease. Banting believed that extracts of the pancreas had not yielded an active hormone because the powerful digestive enzymes of the pancreas must be breaking down the islet hormone during the extraction process. If the ducts were first tied off, the digestive portion of the pancreas would shrivel and stop producing its digestive juices. Then the hormone could be extracted without being destroyed in the process.

To test his idea, Banting needed a laboratory. He went to the chief of biochemistry at the University of Toronto, Professor John J. R. Macleod, to ask for support. At first Macleod refused because funds were scarce. But Banting was persuasive, and he was given a lab and a graduate student named Charles Best to help with the experiments.

Banting and Best removed the pancreases of several experimental dogs. They injected extracts from these organs into the veins of normal dogs. The dogs' blood sugar levels fell. Next the researchers injected the extract into dogs previously made diabetic by removal of the pancreas. Their blood sugar level fell, too! In fact, if enough of the extract was injected, the blood sugar level dropped below normal. Banting and Best wanted to call their hormone extract

Charles Best and Frederick Banting worked together to discover insulin, a hormonal extract from the pancreas.

"isletin," but Professor Macleod insisted that the older name insulin be used.

Banting and Best tried insulin injections on human patients at Toronto General Hospital in 1921. Their first patient was a fourteen-year-old boy named Leonard Thompson. His diabetes had been diagnosed two years before, and doctors had used the only treatment they knew of—a starvation diet of only 450 calories a day. The boy was still alive, but just barely; he weighed only seventy-five pounds. The insulin injections brought his blood sugar level down dramatically. He was able to eat a more normal diet, gained weight, and lived to maturity.

Banting presented a paper on his discovery at the 1921 meeting of the Association of American Physicians, and interest in insulin grew. Macleod assigned his whole staff to work on the problems of isolating insulin and experimenting with it. At first it took half a pound of steer pancreas to produce enough insulin to treat one patient for two weeks. But Best developed methods for large-scale production. Soon commercial manufacturers were producing supplies of the hormone for doctors to use on diabetic patients all around the world.

The 1923 Nobel Prize in Medicine or Physiology was awarded to Banting and Macleod for the insulin breakthrough. Banting was furious. He and Charles Best had done all the work on the basic discovery, yet Best was not even mentioned in the award. At first Banting refused to accept the prize, but eventually he did, and he immediately gave half of his $25,000 share of the award to Best.

Charles Best and Frederick Banting in 1921 with the first diabetic dog to be kept alive with insulin.

The Insulin Revolution

The insulin breakthrough marked a turning point in the treatment of diabetes. Before insulin was isolated, the only approach that was even partially effective was a severely restricted diet. Patients following it had a miserable existence. One twelve-year-old boy grew so desperate that he ate his toothpaste and his pet canary's birdseed. Even this near-starvation diet merely prolonged the lives of juvenile diabetics for only a few years. But with insulin, juvenile diabetics could hope to grow to adulthood, and all diabetics could eat enough food so that they no longer looked like living skeletons.

For a while after Banting's and Best's discovery, research on diabetes stood still. In the excitement of the insulin breakthrough, people assumed that diabetes was cured and needed no further attention. The hormone of the alpha cells, glucagon, was discovered two years after Banting and Best isolated insulin, but then it was largely ignored for five decades. Research efforts were concentrated mainly on developing purer and more effective variations of insulin.

Slowly, however, dissatisfaction grew. People with Type II diabetes may not be helped by injected insulin. Moreover, some people are not willing to submit to a routine of injecting themselves every day, or are too old, feeble, or blind to do so. It is also difficult to get the dose of insulin just right, and taking too much or too little can be dangerous. So gradually researchers began to look again for better ways of treating diabetes.

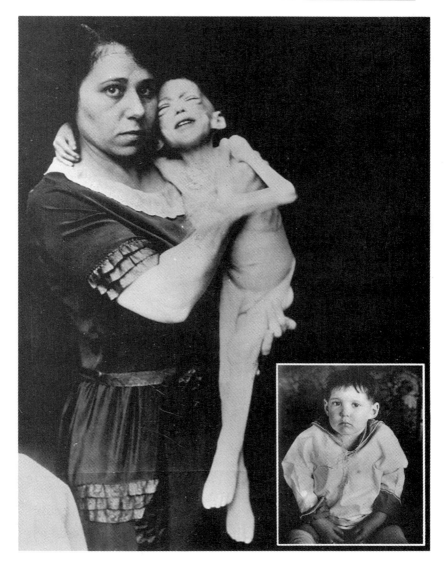

An early insulin success: Diabetes had brought this three-year-old boy close to death. But after two months of treatment his weight increased from an emaciated fifteen pounds to a healthy twenty-nine pounds.

Alternative Treatments

Again a key discovery was made by taking advantage of a lucky accident. In 1948 French researchers R. Jonbon and A. L. Loubatières, of the Institute of Biology at Montpellier, were testing sulfa drugs for typhoid fever. One of the compounds they were using produced an unexpected reaction in rats: it lowered their blood sugar levels. Follow-up studies led to a family of oral hypoglycemic drugs called sulfonylureas. (Hypoglycemic drugs lower the blood sugar level.) Some had too many bad side effects, but others have found use in the treatment of Type II diabetes.

Synthetic Insulin

In 1955 Frederick Sanger, a brilliant biochemist from Cambridge, England, completed a ten-year effort to work out the exact order of all fifty-one amino acids in the insulin molecule and the way they are linked together in two chains. (In 1958 he received a Nobel Prize for this accomplishment.) Once scientists know the chemical structure of a substance, they can think about the possibility of making it. The idea of manufacturing synthetic insulin was especially attractive. The insulin used to treat diabetes came from the pancreas of cattle and hogs as a by-product of their slaughter for meat. But the supply of livestock was shrinking, and the number of diabetics was growing.

In the mid-1960s, three separate groups, working independently, announced the synthesis of insulin. But their techniques were too complicated and expensive to use for mass production.

By the early 1980s scientists had developed more effective ways of making human insulin. Researchers at Squibb-Novo came up with a semisynthetic form. They started with pork insulin, which differs from the human hormone by just one amino acid, and changed that amino acid chemically to the one in human insulin.

Meanwhile, other researchers were using bacteria as miniature "factories" to produce human insulin. Using an approach called the recombinant DNA technique, the hereditary instructions for producing insulin were inserted into the bacteria, which then produced the human protein. Bacteria are microscopic, but they can be grown in huge numbers in tanks, producing pounds or even tons of tailor-made biochemicals. In 1978 a team of researchers at Harvard University and the Joslin Diabetes Center in Boston, led by geneticist Walter Gilbert, announced that they had used recombinant DNA techniques to synthesize rat insulin. Later that same year, researchers at the City of Hope Medical Center in Duarte, California, produced human insulin in the same way. By 1983 recombinant human insulin was available for use by diabetics.

3

What Is Type I Diabetes?

When Gary Krajewski was ten, he suddenly started losing weight. Within a few months he dropped from a husky 117 pounds to only 85 pounds. He felt tired and run-down. He was constantly thirsty, and he kept asking for candy and other sweets. When Gary's worried parents took him to the doctor, his problem was quickly diagnosed: He had diabetes.

LeeAnn Redfern, one of the nurses who helped to teach Gary how to keep his diabetes under control, knew just how he felt. She was diagnosed with the disease when she was eighteen.

Kathy Konopack, a young mother in a nearby town, supervises her seven-year-old son David when he gives himself insulin injections to keep his diabetes under control. "It doesn't affect me the way it might affect other mothers to see him give himself shots," she comments, "because I know that if he didn't he wouldn't be here." Kathy has diabetes, too, diagnosed when she was a child. Like his mother, David has adjusted to the routine and is living an active life. "David plays baseball, plays with all the other kids, and we go bowling every week," Kathy says.[1]

The Sugar-Urine Disease

The name "diabetes mellitus" describes two striking symptoms of the disease. People with uncontrolled diabetes usually have a constant, urgent thirst. Though they drink huge quantities of liquids, the fluid seems to run right through them, for they also have a continual need to urinate. Indeed, it often seems that more fluid comes out than went in. So the first part of the name, meaning a siphon or drain, seems quite appropriate.

The urine of a person with diabetes contains sugar, which is the reason for the "mellitus" part, from the Latin word for honey. Most people today just talk about "diabetes," but physicians prefer to use its more precise, full name, diabetes mellitus. In this way they avoid confusion with another much rarer disease called diabetes insipidus, in which great quantities of urine are also produced, but it does not contain sugar.

There are actually two main types of diabetes mellitus. Type I diabetes used to be called "juvenile diabetes," because it most often (but not always) occurs in children, teenagers, and young adults. This form is also called insulin-dependent diabetes mellitus (IDDM), because the bodies of people with this condition produce little or no insulin, and they must receive insulin injections every day in order to live. Type II diabetes or non-insulin-dependent diabetes (NIDDM) usually strikes people after the age of thirty-five or forty. These people's bodies do produce insulin, but their body cells cannot use it properly. This kind of diabetes can generally be controlled with diet and exercise, or with drugs that lower the amount of sugar in the blood.

Type I Diabetes

About 1.4 million Americans suffer from insulin-dependent diabetes.[2] The problem is usually discovered when the condition is very serious. It often begins quite suddenly. The person may feel fine, and then, with hardly any warning, falls so seriously ill that emergency hospitalization may be necessary.

At first, a person may overlook some of the symptoms of diabetes or think they are due to something else. Reaching for that extra bottle of Coke, one might think, "It certainly is hot today!" A person with a sudden need to urinate more than usual might pass it off with the thought, "I shouldn't have had that extra glass of milk before bedtime." If a child suddenly begins wetting the bed, parents are more likely to wonder about emotional problems than to suspect diabetes. Taken together, though, these symptoms spell out a very clear warning. Since each of us has about one chance in five of developing diabetes at some time in life, it is a warning we should all learn to read.

Who Gets Type I Diabetes?

Although Type I diabetes usually first appears in children, teens, or young adults, it can occur in tiny babies or in middle-aged or older adults. It strikes both sexes and is found equally among males and females. It is rare among Asians, Africans, and Native Americans.

What causes diabetes? Why can't the body handle the sugars it needs to provide energy? What other effects does the disease produce? Before examining what goes wrong in the body of someone with diabetes, we need to know something about how the healthy body works.

The Factory Inside Us

Your body is a miniature chemical factory. While you sit reading this book, countless numbers of tiny production lines are busily turning out the chemicals you need to breathe, read, turn the page, and think.

Like any factory, the body needs fuel and raw materials. The foods we eat supply them. Starches, such as those found in potatoes and bread, are digested into sugars, which can pass easily through the walls of the digestive tract into the bloodstream, and then into the body cells. (Both starches and sugars belong to the group of foodstuffs called carbohydrates.) Proteins, the main ingredients in meat and fish, are digested into smaller units called amino acids. Fats and oils are broken down into their component parts, called fatty acids and glycerol.

All three types of foodstuffs—carbohydrates, proteins, and fats—can be used as fuel by the body. But if there is enough sugar available, the body will generally use that as fuel in preference to proteins and fats. Proteins are the main building materials of the body; they form the bulk of muscles and skin. The brain, nerves, and other body tissues contain large amounts of fats.

Generally the body uses what food it needs and stores any extras. Sugars are stored in the liver and muscles in the form of a starch called glycogen. Proteins may be changed into sugars or fats for storage, or may be broken down and sent out of the body in the urine. Fats are stored in "fat depots" in various parts of the body, for example, the belly and buttocks. If food does not contain enough materials to support all the body's activities, the body will live off its reserves, drawing out sugar from the glycogen in the liver and muscles, then taking fat from the fat depots, and, if necessary, even pulling proteins out of the muscles.

Scientists call the sum total of all the chemical reactions that go on in the body metabolism. Chemicals called hormones act on each other and on the cells of the body to control the body's metabolism. Hormones are produced by the body's endocrine glands, which send their secretions directly into the bloodstream to coordinate many activities in the body.

The Pancreas

The gland most involved in the body's handling of sugar is the pancreas. Shaped rather like a fish, it lies across the middle of the abdomen, nestled behind the stomach and liver. The pancreas is both an endocrine and a digestive gland. Most of it produces digestive juices that empty into the intestine through ducts and help us to digest our food.

Scattered through the pancreas are small masses of tissue that look quite different from the rest of the organ when they are viewed under a microscope. These small "islands" are the endocrine portion of the gland. There are more than 100,000 of these islets of Langerhans.

The islets themselves contain several different kinds of hormone-producing cells. Two important ones are the alpha cells and beta cells, and they produce two different hormones: insulin, the hormone made and released by the beta cells, and glucagon, the hormone produced by the alpha cells. Both work to control the body's use of sugar (which scientists call sugar metabolism), but their effects are almost exactly opposite.

Insulin is secreted when the amount of sugar in the blood rises, and it works to lower the blood sugar level in a number of ways. Insulin makes it easier for the simple sugar glucose to pass into body cells. It helps some cells, such as those of the liver, to change glucose into the starch glycogen and put it away in storage. Other cells are prompted by insulin to change glucose into fatty acids, which are also stored. Insulin also helps the cells to build amino acids into proteins, and keeps them from converting amino acids and fatty acids into sugars.

Glucagon is secreted when the blood sugar level falls, and it works to put more sugar into the blood. Glucagon makes liver cells break down some of their stored glycogen into glucose. It also aids in converting amino acids and fatty acids into glucose. Thus, glucagon and insulin work like two people sitting on opposite ends of a seesaw. If the blood sugar level goes up too high, the amount of insulin rises and pushes the blood sugar down. If the blood sugar levels fall too low, glucagon boosts it back up again. Together, the two hormones keep the amount of glucose in the blood moving up and down within a narrow range.

The "Normal" Blood Sugar Level

What is the "right amount" of glucose in the blood? In fact, what is sugar doing in the blood in the first place, and why does the body need a complicated system of hormones to keep it in balance?

Glucose is the favored energy fuel for most cells of the body. It is carried throughout the body by the blood. A relatively small amount of sugar can supply the needs of the trillions of cells in the human body. All the blood of an average-sized adult man usually contains just about a teaspoon of glucose. But a person's blood sugar level is not the same all the time. It goes up shortly after a meal, when foods from the digestive tract are passing into the bloodstream; and it goes down when a person hasn't eaten for a long time. During your long night's sleep, you don't eat anything, so your blood sugar level is generally lowest just before breakfast. (This is called your fasting blood glucose level.)

In a healthy person, the swings in blood sugar level are not permitted to go very far. When sugar floods into the blood after a meal, the pancreas quickly secretes insulin, which helps the body cells get the sugar tucked away into storage. When a person has fasted or is starved, glucagon keeps the blood sugar level from falling too low. In a healthy person, the blood sugar level rarely rises above a concentration of 160 milligrams in each 100 milliliters of blood (which is expressed as 160 mg%), even after a meal, or falls below 60 mg%, even during a fast. The normal fasting blood sugar level ranges from 70 to 120 mg%, or about 80 mg% on the average.

What Goes Wrong

Normally, the pancreas sends out just enough of the right hormone to keep the blood glucose level within the narrow range of "just enough." But in diabetes something has gone wrong. The blood sugar rises far above the normal limit—perhaps up to 200, 300, or even 1000 mg% or more. This condition (too much sugar in the blood) is called hyperglycemia.

Damage to the beta cells is usually the cause of Type I diabetes. Ironically, scientists believe that islet cells are destroyed by the person's own body in an autoimmune response. Normally the body's immune system works to defend it against foreign invaders, such as disease germs. Its weapons include proteins called antibodies, which attack foreign substances. But in Type I diabetes the body produces antibodies that attack and destroy the beta cells in the pancreas. The pancreas can no longer produce enough insulin to keep the blood sugar level in check.

Effects on the Kidneys

All the blood in the body is continually filtered through the kidneys. These two large, bean-shaped organs get rid of many of the body's waste products and poisons by producing urine. Blood cells and large molecules such as proteins are held back by the kidneys. There is a continual trading of chemicals back and forth. If there is too much of something in the blood—a salt, for example—the excess passes into the urine. If there is only just enough of a substance, or a shortage of it, the kidneys will return it to the blood.

In a healthy person, there is just the right amount of glucose in the blood, so the kidneys hold it all back. Normally there is no sugar in the urine. But when the blood sugar level rises beyond about 180 mg%, the renal threshold, the excess sugar begins to "spill" over into the urine, like extra water over a dam. The presence of glucose in the urine is called glucosuria.

There must always be enough water in the urine to keep irritating and poisonous wastes well diluted. As the amount of glucose spilling into the urine increases, the urine becomes more concentrated. So the kidneys must pass out more water to keep the urine diluted enough. Then the body becomes dehydrated, and the person becomes thirsty. With all the extra water flowing out through the kidneys, minerals are washed out too, along with proteins and fats, which are not normally excreted by the kidneys. So a person with uncontrolled diabetes begins to lose weight.

Meanwhile, despite all that sugar floating around in the blood, the person is unable to use sugar effectively as a fuel for normal body activities. Chemical distress signals are sent out by the hungry cells, and a metabolic switch-over begins. The body begins to raid its fat stores for energy fuel, and it may even begin to pull protein from the muscles. (That's like a family who have run out of fuel oil chopping up their furniture and burning it in the fireplace to keep warm—it may solve the problem temporarily, but it creates even worse problems later on.)

When fats are broken down for energy, chemicals called ketone bodies are formed as by-products. These build up in the blood and spill over into the urine; they may give the breath a distinctive "fruity," acetone odor. Ketone bodies are somewhat acid, and they upset the acid balance of the blood. This is a delicate balance, and it is normally maintained within very narrow limits. Too much acid can poison or even kill body cells. If too much fat must be used to provide energy because there is not enough insulin to allow the use of glucose for fuel, a state called ketoacidosis develops. The person may lose consciousness, may go into a coma, and—if not rescued by prompt medical treatment may die.

Complications of Diabetes

Baseball fans all around the world know that Jackie Robinson, the first African-American player to break into the Major Leagues, was one of baseball's greatest superstars. But few realize he had diabetes.

At first Jackie and his doctors were able to keep his disease under good control, and it hardly bothered him at all. But problems developed. First he developed an infection in a knee that he had once injured sliding into second base. The

31

Diabetes did not stop Jackie Robinson from becoming a baseball superstar. Despite this disease, he was the first African American to enter the Major Leagues.

infection spread through his body, and Jackie almost died before antibiotics finally brought it under control.

In later years diabetes affected Jackie's nerves and blood pressure, causing burning pains in his legs that eventually made him give up playing golf. Tiny blood vessels in his eyes began to bleed. Though doctors fought the damage with the newest techniques of laser surgery, Jackie lost the sight of one eye, then of the other. Then three heart attacks struck within four years; the last one killed him at the age of fifty-three.

Today very few people die of diabetic coma, but the disease can cause a number of serious complications that can limit and shorten life. People with diabetes are more likely than the average person to develop ailments of the heart and blood vessels, kidney problems, nerve damage, and eye problems, for example. (Diabetes is currently the leading cause of blindness in the United States.)

Fortunately, there are a number of ways of diagnosing diabetes early, as well as treatments that can help to prevent its disabling and life-threatening effects in many patients. In 1993 diabetes specialists and their patients were excited by the report on a large-scale, federally sponsored study. The results of this ten-year study showed that keeping the blood sugar level under careful, tight control could prevent most of the damaging complications of the disease.

4

What Is Type II Diabetes?

Forty-six-year-old Tony Paolo thought at first that he had the flu. He had been leading an active life, but now he felt tired all the time. He found that he had to go to the bathroom much more often than usual, and he couldn't seem to quench his thirst, no matter how much fluid he drank. He lost twelve pounds, and his vision started blurring. When he consulted a doctor, tests quickly showed that he had diabetes.[1]

Among the fourteen million Americans with diabetes, only about 10 percent have IDDM (Type I diabetes).[2] The far more common forms of non-insulin-dependent diabetes (NIDDM) or Type II diabetes usually strike people after the age of thirty-five or forty—and they strike mainly people who are overweight. More than 12.5 million Americans have

Type II diabetes, and as many as half of them don't even know they have it.

Non-insulin-dependent diabetes can go on for years before it is detected. Many people first discover they have diabetes when a routine medical checkup shows sugar in the urine. They may have such mild cases that there have been no symptoms at all.

When symptoms do appear, they may be similar to those of Type I diabetes—excessive urination, extreme thirst and hunger, for example. A person with Type II diabetes may also have frequent infections and find that cuts and bruises are slow to heal. Blurred vision is another common symptom. (Fluctuations in the blood sugar level may affect the flow of fluid into and out of the eyeballs, causing them to swell or contract and thus change the way images are focused on the retina.)

Other Forms of Diabetes

Some people have high sugar levels only at times of great stress, or during an illness. When tested at other times, they seem perfectly normal. This condition is called "prediabetes" or previous abnormality of glucose tolerance (PrevAGT). Everything may go back to normal, or the disease may crop up in a more serious form later. A person with this type of "hidden" diabetes may only need to eat a sensible diet, get plenty of exercise, and have regular checkups to make sure the condition has not progressed.

Some women develop high blood sugar while they are

pregnant, then return to normal after the baby is born. This condition is referred to as gestational diabetes mellitus (GDM) (gestation is another word for pregnancy). Women who have abnormal blood sugar levels during pregnancy have an increased risk for complications during pregnancy, and also for developing real diabetes later.

Some people have higher than normal blood glucose levels, but not high enough to be classified as diabetic. These people are said to have impaired glucose tolerance, because the body is not using sugar properly. Impaired glucose tolerance may persist for many years; some people may then develop diabetes, and some return to normal.

Who Gets Type II Diabetes?

Type II diabetes occurs in both sexes, but women who have had a lot of children and those who have had unusually large babies seem to face a special risk. People who have relatives with diabetes (especially Type II diabetes) have a greater chance of developing the disease themselves.

Diabetes affects all the peoples of the earth, with a few exceptions: It is extremely rare among Eskimos, for example. In the United States, minority groups seem to be especially hard hit: Type II diabetes, the more common form, occurs about 60 percent more often in blacks than in whites, and its prevalence is also very high among Hispanic populations and certain Native American tribes such as the Pimas and Papagos.

The probability of getting Type II diabetes increases with

age. The risk also increases with the amount of excess weight. At least three-quarters of the people who develop diabetes in middle or old age are overweight. Yet not all (or even most) overweight people develop diabetes.

What Goes Wrong

Although Type I diabetes is caused by damage to the beta cells of the pancreas, so that they cannot secrete enough insulin, some people with very serious cases of diabetes have beta cells that look perfectly normal. Tests of their blood show plenty of insulin—more than enough, it would seem, to keep the sugar metabolism running smoothly. Yet they too suffer from hyperglycemia.

High blood sugar could result if the pancreas is producing normal amounts of insulin, but the body's needs for the hormone become far higher than normal and the gland cannot keep up. This might happen when people overeat to an extreme degree, flooding their bodies with more carbohydrates than their system can handle. (In general, any diet that results in a gain in weight will increase one's chances of developing diabetes. A diet that causes weight reduction will decrease one's chance of developing diabetes, or, if it is already present, will make it less severe.)

In some cases of diabetes, the insulin that the pancreas produces does not work properly. This may happen for several reasons. For example, the body normally produces a chemical called insulinase, which breaks down excess insulin when its job is done. If too much insulinase is produced, the insulin will be destroyed before it has had a chance to lower the body's blood sugar level. Sometimes the body produces antibodies against insulin, in much the same way it makes them against disease germs. These anti-insulin antibodies may attack insulin or attach themselves to its molecules so that the hormone cannot work on the cells. Certain drugs, including cortisone, prednisone, contraceptive pills, nicotinic acid, and some diuretics (drugs that are used to rid the body of excess fluids), can interfere with the action of insulin.

Diabetes may also result from hormone disorders, in which the body produces too much glucagon or too much of another pancreatic hormone called somatostatin. This hormone, secreted by the delta cells in the islets, helps to regulate the secretion of both glucagon and insulin.

In non-insulin-dependent diabetes, insulin may not be able to allow glucose to pass into the cells effectively because something is wrong with the outer surface of the cells. Researchers have found that insulin normally reacts with specific chemicals, called receptors, on the cells' outer membranes. If there are not enough of these receptors, or if they become less receptive to insulin, the hormone will not be able to help glucose get into the cells. This condition is called insulin resistance.

5

What Causes Diabetes?

Harvey made the second-string football team in his junior year in high school, and he hoped that he'd be playing on the starting team when he was a senior. But then he got sick. For a month he felt exhausted, and he lost eighteen pounds. He was constantly thirsty. His worried mother took him to the doctor, and after blood and urine tests Harvey found himself checked into the hospital. The diagnosis was diabetes. At first he panicked. But the doctor assured him, "You can control this disease and be a winner." What about football? "I'm sorry," the doctor advised, on the basis of medical policy at that time, "no contact sports. Try tennis." Harvey's mind was filled with anger and painful questions as he thought about his future in a life that had changed so suddenly. How would the guys on the team act toward him?

What about his girlfriend? Would everybody feel sorry for him? Why had he suddenly become different?

Harvey eventually adjusted to the routine of keeping a check on his sugar levels and giving himself insulin shots. He learned to play tennis, built a successful career, and even traveled to exotic places around the world. He lost his college sweetheart when her parents refused to let her marry a man with diabetes, but later he fell in love again, married, and raised three healthy children.[1]

In the years since Harvey first learned he had diabetes, scientists have learned a great deal about the disease. They do not have all the answers yet, but they know much more about how and why diabetes develops, and why one person gets it but another does not.

Why Diabetes Occurs

In Chapter 3 we discussed what happens in the body to produce the symptoms of diabetes. But describing *how* diabetes may develop is not the same as explaining *why* it happens. It is believed that diabetes has not one cause, but, rather, many causes. Some of these are still unknown, though researchers have already discovered a number of clues. Some of the newest findings have turned many old ideas about the condition upside down.

Heredity

For many years doctors have noticed that diabetes often occurs in families. So scientists believed it was a hereditary disease: If a person inherits "diabetes genes" from his or her parents, he or she will eventually get the disease. But genetic studies have indicated that heredity is not the whole story.

Identical twins share exactly the same genes. So if Type I diabetes is inherited, you would expect that if one twin has insulin-dependent diabetes, the other will have it as well. Researchers were surprised to find that this was not so. Dr. Priscilla White and other scientists at the Joslin Diabetes Center in Boston surveyed people with Type I diabetes who were identical twins and found that only about half of the other twins also had the disease. Even 50 percent, of course, is still much higher than the probability that two unrelated people will have diabetes (just 0.3 percent).[2]

Quite a different result was found when the researchers studied identical twins who developed diabetes at the age of forty or later. If one of those twins had diabetes, then 90 percent of the time the other did, too. So it seems that heredity may indeed be a major factor in cases where diabetes appears in middle and old age.

Researchers now believe that there is not a single "diabetes gene;" instead, a number of genes are involved, and they interact with one another and can be affected by many things. It is also believed that what is inherited is a predisposition to get the disease, not the disease itself. Thus diabetes can be thought of as a loaded gun—those who are born with it must have something pull the trigger in order for the disease to develop.

A Viral Cause?

In 1864, a Norwegian scientist reported that a patient developed diabetes after getting the mumps. Since then, more evidence has been found to link Type I diabetes with infectious diseases. Medical workers have noticed that diabetes in children, normally a rather rare disease (though it is growing ever more common), tends to occur in clusters. A number of cases will suddenly crop up in a particular area, and these outbreaks sometimes follow an epidemic of a viral disease, such as mumps or rubella (German measles). Coxsackie viruses (common viruses that can cause colds and intestinal infection) have also been implicated.

New cases of Type I diabetes seem to occur seasonally: most in the autumn and winter and least in the summer and spring—just like the incidence of many viral diseases. In some cases, diabetes "epidemics" follow virus epidemics closely; in others, there is a period of about three or four years between the outbreak of the viral disease and the appearance of diabetes symptoms.

Of course, it might be that the extra stress of the viral disease is just too much for a person who happens to have a weak pancreas, and the gland breaks down when the body is besieged by the disease germs. But researchers began to wonder whether the viral illness might actually damage the pancreas. Viruses might invade the pancreas and destroy the beta cells. Or there might be a more indirect effect, involving a mistaken attack by the body's own defenses. The virus particles might happen to be chemically similar to part of the

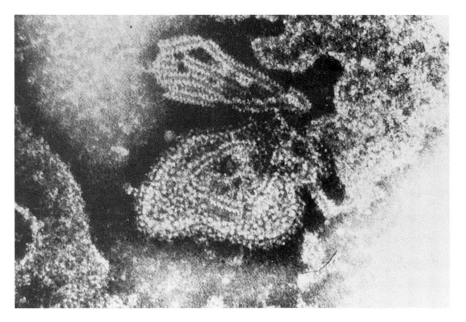

Evidence has been found which links Type I diabetes with infectious diseases, such as the mumps virus pictured above.

surface of the beta cells. (This kind of accidental similarity of environmental proteins to body biochemicals is called molecular mimicry.) Then antibodies produced by the body to attack the viruses would also attack and destroy beta cells. In any case, as beta cells are destroyed, the amount of insulin produced is greatly reduced. When 80 to 90 percent of the beta cells have been destroyed, the symptoms of diabetes develop quite suddenly.

There is a good deal of evidence to support the molecular mimicry theory. People with insulin-dependent diabetes usually make little or no insulin, and examinations of tissue from their pancreases show that beta cells have indeed been destroyed. Antibodies against these cells can be found circulating in the blood of a person with Type I diabetes. In fact, antibodies against one beta cell substance (glutamic acid decarboxylase, or GAD) may appear years before diabetes develops. Now researchers have confirmed that GAD is remarkably similar to a protein of the Coxsackie viruses.

All children catch viral diseases, usually quite a number of them during the growing years. Yet most children *don't* develop diabetes. What determines that a virus infection will cause diabetes in one child, while another child will suffer the same infection and recover with full health?

If insulin-dependent diabetes is indeed an autoimmune disease—one in which the body makes antibodies against a virus that will also attack its own body cells—then a child who does not develop diabetes after a virus infection may just have been lucky enough not to produce those destructive antibodies. Each person produces his or her own unique antibodies against any particular germ or chemical. So some children may produce antibodies that simply cure them of the viral infection without affecting the pancreas.

Another possibility is that a person may inherit a pancreas or an immune system that is particularly susceptible to molecular mimicry. Researchers have found that most people with Type I diabetes have specific types of chemicals on the surfaces of their beta cells that are not usually found in other people. These cell-surface chemicals, which are hereditary, might be the chemicals against which a person's body makes antibodies when viruses attack. (In Type II diabetes, this sort of correlation with special cell-surface chemicals is not seen.)

Although viruses may be implicated in Type I diabetes, this does not mean that diabetes is a contagious disease, like colds or mumps or TB. There is no "diabetes virus," and you can't catch diabetes by talking to, touching, or even kissing someone who has diabetes.

The Milk Theory

Viruses aren't the only suspected environmental trigger. In the early 1980s Canadian researchers at the Hospital for Sick Children in Toronto found that rats and mice from specially bred diabetes-prone strains did not develop the disease unless they were given cow's milk during the first few weeks of life. The rats that developed diabetes had high concentrations of antibodies in their blood against a protein in cow's milk, bovine serum albumin (BSA). Some children with diabetes have antibodies to this protein, too. Moreover, the researchers found that the antibodies against BSA also bind to a protein on the surface of beta cells.[3]

The researchers believe that the cow's milk protein may provoke an autoimmune attack against a look-alike protein in the beta cells, causing a slow destruction of pancreas cells, and, ultimately, diabetes. They believe that only children genetically at risk can be affected, and that exposure must occur in the early months of life when the immune system is still learning the difference between its own molecules and foreign ones. (Breast-feeding, on the other hand, seems to protect against diabetes.)

The evidence is not yet conclusive. Scientists will have more concrete data at the conclusion of a ten-year international study that is following children who do and do not drink cow's milk before the age of nine months.

The Trigger for Type II Diabetes

Some researchers are not convinced that environmental factors are involved at all in causing Type I diabetes. Even identical twins can have differences in their immune systems that determine whether or not diabetes will appear, points out Dr. Mark Atkinson of the University of Florida in Gainesville.[4] But there seems little doubt that environmental factors do play a major role in the development of Type II diabetes.

Being overweight seems to be one of the most important factors in the development of diabetes in adults. People generally become overweight by overeating—taking in more food than the body needs to fuel its activities. The rise in blood glucose after each heavy meal stimulates the secretion of insulin. Years of overeating may overload the beta cells of a diabetes-prone person, and they may lose their ability to produce insulin.

In addition, researchers have found that the body's need for insulin rises when a person is overweight. As extra insulin circulates in the blood, body cells begin to tear down some of their surface insulin receptors. As the number of insulin receptors decreases, the circulating insulin becomes less effective, and a rising blood sugar level signals the pancreas to produce even more insulin—which in turn stimulates a further decrease in cellular insulin receptors.

These effects can be reversed to some degree. When obese people with diabetes manage to bring their weight down by strict dieting and exercise, the symptoms of the disease may disappear.

6
Testing and Treatment

Doctors at the Joslin Diabetes Center are used to dealing with reactions of worry and shock when they deliver the news that tests are positive for diabetes. But the reaction of one patient really surprised them. He was a prominent sportscaster, and he seemed delighted when he heard the news. "Why are you so happy?" his puzzled doctor asked. "Oh," the sportscaster replied, "I felt miserable for so long. I thought I had some hopeless condition for which there would be no help. I am so happy to have something which can be treated!"[1]

The Diagnosis

How do you know if you have diabetes? A variety of tests are used, for many different purposes. There are quick and easy tests suitable for screening large groups of the population. For example, the doctor may test a urine specimen during a routine medical checkup even if there is no particular reason to suspect diabetes.

One problem with using urine tests to screen for new cases of diabetes is that a person's blood sugar level must be fairly high before any glucose will spill over into the urine. Some people's kidneys will tolerate rather large amounts of sugar in the blood before passing it into the urine. Other people may have sugar in the urine because their kidneys will tolerate only a small amount of sugar in the blood, but turn out to have perfectly normal blood sugar levels. So positive urine sugar tests only indicate the *possibility* of diabetes. They should be followed up by blood tests.

More complicated tests provide more information: whether diabetes is present, how serious the condition is, and what kind of diabetes it is. Such tests are used when a doctor already suspects that a person has diabetes. They provide information that helps the doctor plan methods of treatment, and they can also be used to check on how well a treatment is working. There are even sophisticated tests that give an idea of whether a person might develop diabetes at some time in the future.

When Diabetes Is Suspected

If the doctor suspects diabetes, because the patient has been experiencing symptoms like unusual thirst, frequent urination, fatigue, and sudden, unexplained weight loss, the glucose levels of the patient's blood must be determined. A blood sugar level of 200 mg% or more in a person with the typical symptoms of diabetes confirms the diagnosis.

When the symptoms are not as obvious, the doctor may run a fasting glucose test. The blood test is done early in the morning before any food has been eaten. Fasting glucose levels under 115 mg% for an adult, or under 140 mg% for a child, are considered normal. If glucose levels are high, the patient will be tested again, often on another day. (A single high result might be due to a laboratory error.)

For adult patients, when the diagnosis is still uncertain, the doctor may administer a glucose tolerance test. First the fasting glucose level is determined, then the patient drinks a measured amount of a concentrated glucose solution. (It tastes so sweet that most people have to struggle to get it all down.) The patient's blood is then tested again at various times after drinking the liquid to see how quickly glucose levels rise, how high they rise, and how long it takes for them to come down again. These results show how well the pancreas can cope with a sugar load. Too high a rise or too slow a fall may be an indication of diabetes. (In a healthy person, the blood sugar level is usually back down to the fasting level within three hours after a meal.)

Once the doctor's suspicions are confirmed, how does he or she figure out which type of diabetes the patient has? "Together with the results of these tests, the patient's age and weight often pretty much tell us which type of diabetes it is," says Dr. Douglas Greene of the University of Michigan

Medical Center. "If someone is young rather than old and lean rather than fat, we suspect Type I disease (IDDM) rather than Type II, whereas we suspect Type II disease (NIDDM) if the patient is heavy and getting along in years."[2] Blood or urine tests for ketones also help doctors make a diagnosis: patients with Type I diabetes often have evidence of ketone buildup, which is much less common in Type II diabetes.

How Diabetes Is Treated

Thirteen-year-old Gary Krajewski has a far stricter routine than most boys his age. He gives himself insulin injections twice a day, and six times each day he pricks his finger to test his sugar level. He has to watch his diet, too. "I was eating a lot of candy before this happened," he says. "I was a basic little kid, ya know?" But Gary is philosophical about the chores of living with Type I diabetes. "I'm probably healthier than most kids," he adds. "I'm not eating that junk food."[3]

Tony Paolo, who learned at forty-six that he had Type II diabetes, also has a strict routine. Three days a week he gets up early to work out. He has thirty pounds to go to get down to the weight his doctor suggested as a goal. That means no splurging at mealtime, either. He weighs out his portion of breakfast cereal, eats low-fat meats, and counts calories all day, trying to stay within a 2,000-calorie limit. At first he checked his blood sugar level twice a day, before breakfast and after dinner, but now he has been able to cut back to twice a week. Tony is glad about that. "You get used to the routine," he says, "but not the pinprick."[4] So far his careful routine is keeping his diabetes under good control, without the need for oral hypoglycemic drugs.

The treatment of diabetes may thus be quite different, depending on the type of disease:

> *Type I diabetes:* Insulin; diet and exercise are also important.

> *Type II diabetes:* Diet and exercise; oral drugs or insulin may also be needed.

Diabetes treatment puts a lot of responsibility on the patient, but typically a whole health-care team is there for help, advice, and support. In addition to the doctor, who prescribes medications, outlines a plan of diet and exercise appropriate for the patient's condition and life-style, and periodically monitors how well the disease is being controlled, the team may also include a dietitian and a diabetes nurse-educator. Medical specialists, such as an ophthalmologist (eye doctor) and a podiatrist (foot doctor), and perhaps a psychiatrist and a social worker, are also available for special needs.

Goals of Diabetes Control

Diabetes treatment programs are aimed at keeping the level of sugar in the blood normal. This will help prevent problems that result from uncontrolled blood sugar levels. In children, the treatment program must also provide for normal growth and development.

Control requires balancing food intake, the amount of exercise, and insulin levels. Generally, food makes glucose

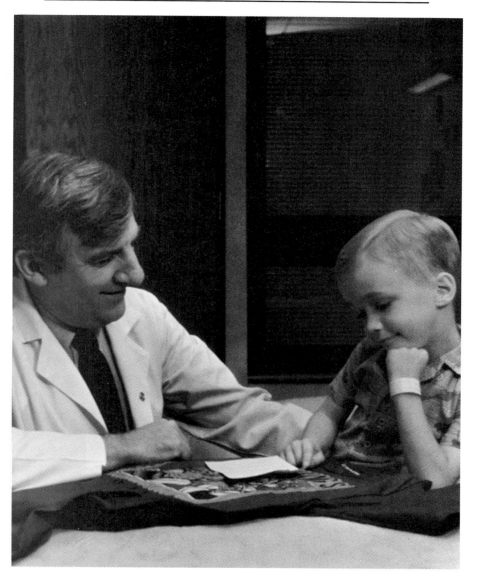

People with diabetes must assume a great deal of responsibility for their own treatment. Doctors generally provide support and advice for the patient and periodically check up on how well the disease is being controlled.

levels rise; exercise and insulin make glucose levels fall. When the body is not producing enough effective insulin, it may have to be supplied by injections, or its production may be stimulated by oral hypoglycemic drugs.

Just how tight a control is needed? Until 1993, that question was open to debate. Some diabetes specialists believed it wasn't realistic to expect the average person with diabetes to be able to keep to the kind of strict routine necessary to keep the blood sugar level normal at all times. They thought that fluctuations were not too significant—as long as they didn't reach the range that might result in ketoacidosis or a hypoglycemic reaction—and all the extra tests and injections that might be necessary to maintain tight control would not be worth the effort. But the report on the ten-year Diabetes Control and Complications Trial (DCCT) changed the diabetes picture dramatically.

The DCCT Results

The massive test, financed by the National Institute of Diabetes and Digestive and Kidney Diseases (NIDDK), began back in 1983, at twenty-nine medical centers in the United States and Canada. A total of 1,441 people with Type I diabetes took part. Their average age at the start of the test was twenty-seven; the group was approximately half men and half women. Some of the test subjects had no signs of complications, but in others there were indications that eye disorders, kidney problems, nerve damage, or other complications were beginning to develop. Each person was assigned randomly to one of two groups.

The first group (the controls) received the diabetes treatment that had been the standard for many years. The IDDM patients typically injected insulin once or twice a day, tested their blood sugar once a day, followed a planned program of diet (including three meals plus three snacks each day) and exercise, and were checked by medical professionals every two or three months.

Patients in the second group (the experimentals) followed a much more aggressive approach to diabetes control. They monitored their blood sugar levels four to seven times a day and fine-tuned their insulin dosages either with three to five injections a day or by using an insulin pump that supplied a continuous flow of insulin into the body. They paid close attention to diet and exercise. The patients were helped by teams of nurses, dietitians, and doctors who called them on the phone at least once a week to check on how things were going and provide any needed advice. The experimental patients also visited a diabetes clinic each month.

The study was intended to go on until 1994, but the results were so striking that the test was stopped a year early so that all people with diabetes could benefit from its findings. "The discovery of insulin was an absolute miracle; this study is in the ball park of comparison," commented NIDDK director, Dr. Phillip Gordon.[5]

Comparisons of the two treatment groups indicated that the "tight-control" program decreased the development of eye problems by 76 percent, cut the rate of severe kidney problems by 35 to 56 percent, and decreased crippling nerve disorders by 60 percent.[6]

There were a few drawbacks. People on the tight-control regimen had about triple the risk of fainting as a result of an insulin reaction, compared to those on the conventional diabetes treatment. And the cost of treatment (typically about $1,500 to $2,000 a year on the conventional regimen) is doubled. But this short-term cost increase is far less than the long-term costs of treating the serious complications that the tight-control treatment can delay or prevent. And most people would say that the increased risk of a hypoglycemic reaction is well worth the benefit of a longer, healthier life.

Does the tight-control regimen add to the burdens of coping with diabetes? Not really, says New Jersey diabetes specialist Dr. Richard Agrin. The aggressive approach has been used for years at the Diabetes Treatment Center at Somerset Medical Center, where he is the medical director. "Our experience is that patients have better control of their disease, and as a result, they also are happier and less anxious," he says. "Aggressive treatment allows them to tailor their treatment to their life-styles instead of adjusting their life-styles to their need for insulin."[7]

The Proper Diet

What is the "right" diet for someone with diabetes? That is a question that has been debated for thousands of years. The diet now recommended for people with diabetes is basically the same as the healthy diet recommended for everyone. It contains about 50 percent carbohydrates (including foods with plenty of natural fiber, such as fruits and whole-grain cereals), about 20 percent proteins, and 30 percent or less fats. People with diabetes should try to avoid refined sugars, such as table sugar, which pass quickly into the blood.

The amount of food that a person with diabetes eats is particularly important, both for those taking insulin and for those being treated with diet alone. There should be enough food to provide nourishment without causing weight gain (except in actively growing children). Obese people need a diet that will help them lose weight, because in Type II diabetes lowering the weight to normal will often decrease or even eliminate the need for any other therapy.

Many people with diabetes go to a dietitian or a nutritionist to help them develop a dietary program. A dietitian may be recommended by a physician or local diabetes group such as the American Diabetes Association.

Helpful diet plans for treating diabetes have been drawn up. These plans operate on the basis of "exchanges," portions of foods that are equivalent in type and amount of nourishment. Substitutions may be made within exchange groups. For example, a person might eat a portion of cereal or spaghetti instead of bread. An ounce of lean beef could be exchanged for an ounce of fish. Some of the equivalents are not so obvious—starchy vegetables like peas, for example, are more similar in nutrient value to breads and cereals than to vegetables like green beans. The diet may allow larger amounts of leafy green vegetables, which are very low in calories and carbohydrates, and high in fiber.

Sugar Substitutes

Some doctors feel that people with diabetes shouldn't use sugar substitutes because they simply maintain their "sweet tooth." If the patients tried eating a more sensible diet, these doctors say, they would soon lose their taste for rich, sweet foods, and that would be a good thing. But some people feel that life just wouldn't be worth living if they couldn't have candy, a soft drink, or some other sweet-tasting treat at least occasionally. And some doctors feel that sugar substitutes are good because they permit people with diabetes, especially young ones, to enjoy some of the same treats as their friends, which can help them feel less "different."

Nutritive sweeteners contain calories, and are usually carbohydrates that end in -ose, such as glucose, fructose, dextrose, and sucrose (sugars), or -ol, such as sorbitol and mannitol (sugar alcohols). They each contain four calories per gram.

Non-nutritive sweeteners provide almost no calories and do not affect blood glucose levels. Saccharin and aspartame (sold under the brand name NutraSweet) are the two major sugar substitutes. Aspartame actually contains the same four calories per gram as do the nutritive sweeteners; however, because it is 180 times sweeter than table sugar, much less has to be used. Saccharin is 300 times sweeter than sucrose and has no calories at all.

Dietetic foods are not necessarily good for people with diabetes. Some contain nutritive sweeteners such as fructose and sorbitol that need to be carefully monitored.

Exercise

People with diabetes are usually encouraged to exercise regularly—which is good advice for most people in general. Exercise reduces the risk of heart disease and hardening of the arteries. It also helps insulin work better. Regular exercise makes body cells respond better to insulin in both Type I and Type II diabetes.

Getting a doctor's advice before starting an exercise program is a good idea, and it is especially important for people with diabetes. If diabetes is not under good control, long exercise sessions could result in the body using fatty acids for energy and producing potentially dangerous ketone bodies. Some people also need to take special care of their feet, or to avoid activities that raise the pressure inside their eyeballs.

Insulin Shots

Diet and exercise are important for everyone who has diabetes. For those with Type II they may be enough to bring the glucose levels into the right balance. But people with Type I diabetes must have injections of insulin to bring their condition under control.

Most people don't like going to a doctor for shots, and the idea of having one or more injections every day (and giving them to yourself!) might seem scary. But people lose the fear of injections when they are given frequently, and daily insulin shots soon become routine.

Giving yourself an injection is really not too hard to do. First, you fill the syringe to the proper dose from the insulin bottle, taking care that no air bubbles remain in the syringe. Then wipe a spot on the skin with a cotton swab dipped in alcohol; this cleans the skin and kills any germs that might cause infection. Then, with the hand not holding the syringe, pinch up the skin into a bulge. (In a muscular area like the thigh, it may be better to stretch the skin out tight rather than pinch it.) Quickly insert the needle into the skin. (The quicker you are, the less it hurts.) Then push the plunger down, injecting all the insulin in the syringe; withdraw the needle carefully; and wipe the skin again with alcohol. Plastic disposable syringes are designed to be used once, then thrown away. (Bacteria could multiply on a dirty syringe, so reusing it could be dangerous.)

There are several new options available for taking insulin. Jet injectors, for example, deliver insulin without a needle, in a tiny pressurized stream that penetrates the skin. An insulin pen looks like a regular pen and contains an injection of insulin.

The belly, buttocks, thighs, and upper arms are the places most often used for insulin injections. (Unlike drug abusers, a person injecting insulin for diabetes does not want to inject the drug into a blood vessel. Injecting it into muscle or fatty tissues allows the insulin to be absorbed slowly, a little at a time, rather than in a big dose all at once.) It is a good idea to rotate the injection sites. Too many injections in the same

Insulin is usually injected into muscular or fatty areas such as the thighs, buttocks, belly, or upper arms. This permits the insulin to be absorbed into the body more slowly.

spot sometimes cause the fat deposits under the skin to be absorbed into the body, producing an unsightly dent in the flesh. Deposits of fat under the skin may also form, causing raised lumps. These effects can usually be avoided by not injecting insulin into the same place more than once every few weeks. Both of these problems are also reduced with the human insulins available today.

Insulin shots twice a day are a rather unnatural way to keep the blood sugar level under control. Medical researchers have been working on devices to deliver insulin in a way that is more like how the normal pancreas releases it—in a small, continuous flow, which is increased when more glucose enters the bloodstream and can be adjusted as needed.

A major advance in this quest was the development of insulin pumps, first introduced in the late 1970s. Today more than 10,000 people with IDDM wear external insulin pumps.[8] A needle is taped in place, and insulin is pumped from a storage container through a plastic tube. The pump delivers insulin continuously, in a tiny flow, which is set by the doctor and adjusted by the user on the basis of frequent blood tests and activities such as exercise. Before meals the user presses a button on the pump to get an extra squirt that will work on the glucose from the food.

Implantable pumps are surgically inserted under the skin of the abdomen. The size of a hockey puck, they include a pump and a reservoir containing enough insulin to last up to several months. The flow rate is set with a radio transmitter. Clinical trials involving 350 people with insulin-dependent diabetes are currently under way in the United States, Canada, and France.

Adjusting the Dose

How do you know how much insulin to inject? The doctor sets the doses and the routine of the injections after a period of trial and gradual adjustment. (The aim is to use the smallest amount of insulin that will keep the blood sugar under good control.) Then the patient may make minor changes in the dose on the basis of daily blood tests and any changes in his or her schedule, or special stress, that may arise. A cold or some more serious illness will make the body require more insulin, while heavy exercise will burn up sugar and decrease the person's insulin requirement. (In fact, he or she may need to take a snack before exercising.)

The size and timing of meals are very important for anyone taking insulin. A healthy pancreas adjusts the amount of insulin it delivers according to the body's needs. More insulin is produced after a large meal or a high-sugar, high-fat dessert; the pancreas cuts back its secretion when a healthy person skips a meal. But someone who takes insulin shots cannot adjust the insulin flow in this way. Once the injection is given, the amount cannot be increased or decreased to meet unexpectedly changing needs.

Types of Insulin

The insulin used to treat diabetes comes from several sources. Beef and pork insulins are isolated from animal pancreases.

Measuring the insulin takes some practice. Here a girl with Type I diabetes prepares her insulin injection while her mother supervises.

Recombinant insulins are produced by genetic engineering and are chemically identical to the natural human hormone.

Some of the insulins used in treating diabetes are modified to make them longer-acting than the natural hormone. The insulins available today come in several main types, which work for different periods of time. They may be used either separately or in various combinations.

Regular or *short-acting insulin* is a pure form of insulin, sometimes called "plain," "clear," "unmodified," or "R." It is quick-acting but its effects do not last long. It starts working within half an hour, has the greatest effect in two to four hours, and is completely gone from the bloodstream within about six hours.

Intermediate-acting insulins (*Lente* and *NPH*) enter the bloodstream about two to four hours after injection, have their peak effect in four to fourteen hours, and last from eighteen to twenty-four hours. (The name *lente* comes from the Italian word for "slow.")

Ultralente or *long-acting insulin* (called *U*) is a very slow-acting form; it takes from four to six hours to begin working, and peaks in fourteen to twenty-four hours. This type of insulin continues to work for thirty-six hours.

Why are there different types? Fast-acting insulin is the best type for bringing a person out of a diabetic coma. But for daily use it is often rather inconvenient, at least by itself—since it lasts such a short time, a number of injections a day would be needed. Some of the longer-acting insulins do last throughout a whole day. But these insulins begin acting so slowly that they could not prevent serious sugar buildups if the user ate a meal at a time when the insulin's action was not at its peak. Using mixtures of insulin can solve the problem—for example, an intermediate-acting insulin can take over when the short-acting form stops working.

Diabetic Emergencies

Hypoglycemia, or insulin reaction: Taking too much insulin, exercising too much without eating, skipping or delaying a meal (or even not eating as much as planned) will mean that there is not enough sugar in the blood to use up the injected insulin. Then the blood sugar level will fall—sometimes to a hypoglycemic level, far below normal. The person may turn pale and feel shaky or dizzy. Arms and hands may feel numb, and there may be a tingling sensation around the mouth. As sensitive brain cells become affected by the lack of sugar, the person may become tired and irritable, feel disoriented, say irrational things, and even act peculiarly. Without prompt treatment, an insulin reaction may lead to convulsions and collapse.

Ketoacidosis (sometimes called diabetic coma): This develops gradually after a number of days of poorly controlled diabetes. Without enough insulin, the body is unable to utilize sugar for energy, so it begins to use stored fats instead. The ketones released when fats are broken down build up in the blood and pass into the urine and breath. These acid ketone bodies act as poisons, and the person may ultimately fall unconscious.

What to do in diabetic emergencies: Both insulin reaction and ketoacidosis are very serious medical emergencies. Their causes are opposite, and they require opposite treatments.

For insulin reaction, immediately provide sugar in the form of two sugar cubes, one-half cup of fruit juice or regular soda (not diet soda!), or the amount of candy equal to six or seven Lifesavers. Within ten minutes the person should feel better. After the insulin reaction is over, additional food such as milk, bread, and crackers should be eaten, and then normal activities can be resumed.

Never try to force any food or drink down the throat of an unconscious person—it might go into the windpipe and cause suffocation. An emergency injection of glucagon can help to bring a person out of a severe insulin reaction. A doctor might also give an intravenous injection of glucose. In any case, speed is important.

Ketoacidosis requires emergency treatment in a hospital. But what if a person with diabetes suddenly collapses, and you are not sure whether the cause is ketoacidosis or insulin shock? What should you do?

When uncertain, treat for an insulin reaction. Hypoglycemia develops so rapidly that quick action may be needed to save the person's life or prevent brain damage. If it turns out that the person was really suffering from ketoacidosis, a little more sugar is not going to make much difference, and there will be time to correct for the mistake with injections of insulin. Call a doctor if the person does not respond to a dose of sugar within ten to fifteen minutes, or falls unconscious.

Oral Hypoglycemic Drugs

In treating Type II diabetes, specialists now advise that a doctor first try a controlled diet and exercise, especially for people who are overweight. If this works, it will keep weight down, and the person's own insulin will be able to keep things running properly, which is the best possible situation.

If diet and exercise don't bring Type II diabetes under control, oral drugs may be tried, either alone or in combination with insulin or other drugs. (Today, 30 to 40 percent of those with Type II diabetes in the United States and as many as 50 percent worldwide use oral hypoglycemic drugs.[9] Insulin may be necessary at the beginning of the treatment program. Eventually it may be possible to change to a program of diet alone. Oral agents are most effective for those whose diabetes began after age forty and who have had diabetes less than ten years.

The oral hypoglycemic drugs used today are chemicals called sulfonylureas. The first to be marketed for the treatment of diabetes was tolbutamide, sold under the trade name Orinase. Today, a second generation of highly effective sulfonylurea drugs is available, including Glucotrol (glipizide), and Diabeta (glyburide), which have fewer side effects. These drugs are not insulin substitutes. They work by stimulating the pancreas to increase its secretion of insulin, and by helping to prevent insulin resistance.

A bad thing about the oral antidiabetic drugs is that they falsely lull people (both doctors and patients) into believing that control of diabetes is easy, and that worrying about diet and control of blood sugar is unnecessary. But diet is even more important for those using oral agents, and it may mean the difference between successful blood glucose management and uncontrolled diabetic complications.

The Importance of Education

The World Health Organization has stated that "education is the cornerstone of diabetic therapy and vital to the integration of the diabetic into society."[10] At the Joslin Diabetes Center, in Bethesda, Maryland, which has treated more than 160,000 children and adults with diabetes, the philosophy is that education about diabetes is not an addition to treatment; it *is* treatment. Learning includes not just knowledge about the disease but also skills and attitudes. Its founder, Dr. Elliott P. Joslin, believed that "the diabetic who knows the most, lives longest!"[11]

7
Living With Diabetes

A group of friends in San Francisco were having a potluck dinner. The hamburgers on the grill smelled delicious, and bowls of salad and fresh corn were already on the table. One of the guests pulled out a small case from his pocket, pricked his finger with a lancet, and placed a drop of blood in a small glucose meter. He shook his head as the display showed a reading of 241. "Too high." Quickly he made some calculations. Drawing up some liquid from a vial into a syringe, he pulled up his shirt, pinched up a fold of skin over his abdomen, and injected his dose of insulin. "I have diabetes," he explained.[1]

"There's nothing quite like diabetes, really," comments Dr. Xavier Pi-Sunyer, president of the American Diabetes Association. "It's a chronic disease you have to think about all the time and one that can give you complications down the line. So you tend to deny it for a while. But what you do today will affect you ten years from now. That's hard for patients to understand."[2]

It is a shock to be told that you have diabetes. And after you get over the first reaction of panic, you realize that there are great adjustments to make. A life of restrictions seems to stretch out ahead, with no end or letup in sight. What will you be allowed to eat? Will you be able to work and play like other people? What about marriage and raising a family? Will you be able to master the techniques of giving insulin injections and counting calories? How much of a dent will they make in the normal routines of living?

For most people with diabetes, the disease need not make much of a change in life-style. Active living is not only possible but desirable. Exercise helps to lower the blood sugar level, and active interests in life keep a person from brooding about a chronic health problem.

Some people are reluctant to tell others that they have diabetes, feeling that it is embarrassing and somehow shameful. Such fears are blown up out of proportion. Very few people would feel any different about you, and most would be sympathetic and helpful. If you are taking insulin, it is important for at least one close friend to know about your condition and to know what to do to help you in case of an insulin reaction.

Self-Monitoring Glucose Levels

People with diabetes routinely test their blood sugar level to monitor how well their condition is being controlled. Checking on the amount of sugar in the blood several times a day helps give a better idea of how much insulin is needed. Keeping blood sugar levels under control can help to prevent or even reverse some long-term complications of diabetes.

In the past, urine tests were commonly used for monitoring diabetes. But this is not the best way to measure glucose levels. If there is glucose in the urine, you don't know when it spilled over. A urine test might be negative when blood glucose levels are actually dangerously high. Urine tests don't tell you how high the blood sugar was, either, and they can't tell you when blood sugar levels are too low.

Fortunately, technology has provided an affordable way to measure blood sugar levels by using devices called blood glucose monitors. You can find out exactly what your blood sugar level is in just a few moments. This makes it possible to adjust food and insulin more appropriately than ever before. Using a monitor regularly can also give a timely warning when an insulin reaction is developing, because the blood test shows when there is too little glucose present.

To test blood sugar, you just prick your finger or earlobe and place a drop of blood onto a chemically sensitive strip. In some systems the strip is compared to a color-coded chart, or it is simply placed into a small portable machine that provides a digital readout of blood sugar levels.

Wearing Medical Identification

Wearing a medical identification bracelet or necklace and/or carrying an identification card can also help in case of an

Blood glucose monitors are used to measure blood sugar levels. This makes it possible to adjust insulin and food intake to suit your body's needs.

emergency. Information on your illness and what to do in case of insulin reaction or ketoacidosis, as well as your name and the name and number of someone to contact, may mean the difference between life and death if you are found unconscious.

A nonprofit organization, Medic-Alert Foundation, can provide you with an identification card or tag, and maintains a central file containing vital information on every case registered with it. This information can be obtained twenty-four hours a day by a collect telephone call.

Marriage and Children

Should people with diabetes marry? Can they hope to raise families of their own? Marriage to someone with diabetes requires some special adjustments that many people have made successfully. It is a matter of being willing to make the effort. The couple should have frank and open discussions beforehand, about what the treatment of the disease entails and the possibility that complications might develop in the future.

Should people with diabetes marry each other? Specialists used to say no, believing there was a high risk that children might inherit the disease. But most young diabetes patients who are thinking about getting married and having children have Type I rather than Type II diabetes. Now that studies have indicated that heredity does not play the major role in this form of the disease it was formerly thought to have, there seems little reason to discourage such marriages. In fact, some counselors suggest that if two people with diabetes marry each

Modern medicine has increased the chances of a woman with diabetes having a healthy child. This woman with Type I diabetes had a successful pregnancy. Here she is holding her two-year-old son, with another baby on the way.

other, they will find it easier to adjust, because both of them already know what living with the disease involves.

Is it safe for people with diabetes to have children? There is no reason why a man with diabetes should not father a child. For a woman the problem is a bit more complicated. Modern treatment methods have greatly increased the chances for a woman with diabetes to bear a normal, healthy child. But the rate of death of babies both before and soon after their birth is still somewhat higher than normal. The disease itself also becomes more difficult to control during pregnancy—the body's need for insulin increases, and the woman must be carefully watched by her doctor to avoid possible complications that might threaten her or her child. Doctors recommend getting the blood sugar level under strict control well before becoming pregnant, and monitoring it carefully during the pregnancy. A pregnant woman with diabetes may have to undergo frequent and expensive tests to determine how well her baby is growing and when it should be delivered.

Work

Bret Michaels, the lead singer of the heavy-metal group Poison, manages to combine the routine of blood tests and insulin shots with a demanding job and an unusual life-style. Michaels was first diagnosed at the age of six, learned to give himself injections at ten, and has been part of a rock band since high school. It's sometimes difficult to mesh eight blood tests and three insulin injections a day with a life of concerts

Bret Michaels of the rock group Poison is taking a moment from rehearsal time to give himself an insulin injection as (from left) Richie Kotzen, Rikki Rockett, and Bobby Dall continue to rehearse.

and partying, with constant travel and irregular hours. Michaels admits that he hasn't always kept to a strict life-style, and there have been some problems along the way. He passed out from an insulin reaction in the middle of a concert one night, in front of 20,000 people at Madison Square Garden. The group had been celebrating the success of its first album, and Michaels was suffering from a hangover and unable to eat after taking his insulin shot. Drinking (which he knows he shouldn't do) makes it harder to control his blood sugar level, and overindulgence has put him in the hospital twice.

On the road in Maine, the rock star discovered a different kind of hazard. A hotel maid pricked her finger on one of his discarded needles. She called the police, who arrested Michaels as a suspected heroin addict. His tour manager brought Michaels' insulin supplies and blood-testing kit over to the station, and he was released just in time to make his concert appearance. Michaels does work out regularly, lifting weights and mountain-biking, and he is careful about his diet. But "I don't let diabetes run my life," he says, and adds, "Most diabetics could never live my erratic life-style."[3]

Some occupations, such as piloting an airplane or driving a bus, may not be open to people with diabetes, especially those who are taking insulin. These restrictions are imposed for safety reasons. Passing out from an insulin reaction at a rock concert may be embarrassing, but in some jobs it would be a disaster. Many people's lives might be endangered if an airplane pilot or bus driver suddenly became unconscious on the job. But with relatively few exceptions people with diabetes are free to take up any occupation they wish.

Insurance companies used to refuse to write life insurance policies on people with diabetes. That made sense when people with the disease generally died within a few years after being diagnosed. But modern treatments have permitted most people with diabetes to live a nearly normal life, and insurance companies have changed with the times. Now life insurance policies are available for people with diabetes, although they may be charged somewhat higher premiums.

Travel

Can you travel if you have diabetes? Certainly. Just make sure you take adequate supplies of insulin, syringes, testing materials, and any other equipment you need. Modern insulin preparations will keep well at room temperature for a month or more, though they should be protected from extremes of heat and cold. (Never ship insulin supplies in the baggage compartment of an airplane, which may become boiling hot or freezing cold.)

If you plan to visit a foreign country, know how to say important phrases like "I have diabetes" and "I need a doctor" in the language of the land, even if you can't say anything else. Another good precaution is to take along a doctor's note stating that you have diabetes and must carry injection equipment to treat your condition—otherwise you might be suspected of being a drug addict or dealer and wind up in jail.

Parties and Dates

The diabetes routines can complicate a social life. Sticking to a strict diet can be hard, especially when you are at a party or on a date. The insulin injections pose additional problems, since the timing of your next shot may be awkward, and you can't miss or even delay a meal.

There are ways of getting around such problems gracefully. For instance, if you know that there will be a long wait for dinner, you can take a little snack beforehand to keep your insulin satisfied. (Be sure to deduct the calories from your meal later.) To avoid overeating without hurting the cook's feelings, eat at least a little of a special dish and say something complimentary like "I really wish I could eat more."

Drinking, Drugs, and Smoking

Some doctors say that people with diabetes should drink no alcohol. Others permit a drink or two. But drinking has some special pitfalls for someone with diabetes. First of all, alcohol has calories, and they count in the diet. In addition, alcohol lowers blood sugar at first. Alcohol also impairs a person's judgment. Dr. Raymond Herskowitz at the Joslin Diabetes Center in Boston points out that teens are more likely to have a serious insulin reaction when they've been drinking. A person who is "high" may not be alert to the warning signs, and other people might mistake the effects of low blood sugar for drunken behavior.

Marijuana, like alcohol, can dull your judgment and make

you forget about eating a meal or taking an insulin injection. Or it may make you so hungry that you forget to stick to your diet.

Cigarettes have been linked with so many damaging effects on the heart, lungs, and other body systems that smoking is not a very good idea for anyone. It is an even worse idea for people with diabetes, who are already at risk for heart disease.

Personal Hygiene

Good tooth care is especially important for people with diabetes. Blood-vessel changes, which are often an early complication of the disease, can promote gum diseases and infections. Up to 20 percent of teenagers with Type I diabetes develop gum diseases and abscesses.[4] But thorough brushing and flossing and regular visits to the dentist can remove the plaque that forms on teeth and help to prevent these problems. Young people with diabetes who watch their diet and are conscientious in caring for their teeth actually have fewer cavities than nondiabetics.

Other aspects of personal hygiene can be important, too. Older people with diabetes need to take very good care of their feet, keeping them clean and inspecting them regularly for injuries. Diabetes can cause nerve damage that blunts the sense of touch; so a person might not notice an injury, and a cut or scratch might become infected. Impaired healing of wounds is typical of uncontrolled diabetes and may lead to serious foot problems unless special care is taken.

Diabetes and Illness

Getting sick can present special problems for someone with diabetes. The stress of an illness can make diabetes symptoms worse, and diabetes can make the illness worse. The person's doctor should be alerted whenever he or she gets sick; tests may have to be taken every few hours and the insulin dosage may need continual readjustment to help keep the blood sugar under control.

The body's needs when recovering from an accident can also increase a person's insulin requirements; frequently, special care is needed after an accident.

Special Teen Problems

The teen years are often the time when parents start allowing a young person with diabetes to take more responsibility for managing the disease. But adolescence is a time of rebellion and mood swings, which may make teens less conscientious about their self-care routine. A certain amount of rebellion is a natural part of growing up. But diabetes control, and maintaining good health, requires following a strict regimen.

Not all teenagers can handle the responsibility. Emergency-room physician Elisabeth Rosenthal recalls a patient during her training who was "every intern's nightmare." At twenty-two, Donna had had diabetes since the age of eight. She often "forgot" to take her insulin on schedule, ate candy bars, and once even used her syringes to inject illegal drugs. She wound up in the emergency room every few months, with some new diabetic emergency. "I'm going to kill her," Dr. Rosenthal recalls muttering to herself when Donna was admitted again in ketoacidosis and with a heart attack as well. "No," she then sighed. "She's going to kill herself."[5]

The teen years are often very difficult for people with diabetes. Experts such as Dr. William Tamborlane, professor of medicine at Yale, point out that diabetes "has more adverse psychological effects than other chronic illnesses, partly because it's so intrusive. It affects every aspect of a teenager's life, including eating, sleeping, and exercise."[6] Dr. Robert Sherwin, professor of pediatrics at Yale University, says that "diabetic teenagers have a chronic illness, one that requires so much attention. And during puberty, that problem is superimposed over the problems of sexual development. The additional problem creates additional difficulties."[7]

Some teens with diabetes have erratic control of their blood sugar. Though parents may be quick to criticize their mood swings and rebellious attitude, it may not always be the teenager's fault. During adolescence, changing hormones affect blood sugar levels, which makes it harder to keep them stable. In addition, blood sugar levels influence how a person feels. High blood sugar can cause teens to feel frustrated and irritable, which may make them less self-motivated and can create a vicious circle. Teenage girls may find that their menstrual cycles greatly alter their insulin needs, making glucose control even more difficult.

8

Preventing Diabetes

When Sean Finley was fourteen, doctors told him he would probably develop diabetes within three years. His sister Stephanie had diabetes, and his parents had read in *Countdown* magazine in 1986 that researchers at Joslin Diabetes Center in Boston were looking for relatives of diabetes patients to undergo special antibody tests that could determine whether other family members might develop diabetes. The Joslin doctors asked Sean if he was willing to become part of a study to test a new method for preventing diabetes, called beta cell rest. Sean would have to take insulin shots twice a day. He was angry at first, but three years later his pancreas was still healthy. "I've changed my mind, definitely," he said. "I'm glad I'm on this. I don't want to have diabetes. Period."[1]

Testing for Diabetes Risk

Ever since scientists discovered that Type I diabetes might be caused by an autoimmune response, researchers have been trying to use this information to identify those who might be at risk for developing the disease. In the 1970s doctors at Middlesex Hospital in London discovered antibodies that attack pancreatic islet cells. These antibodies appear in the blood long before the disease begins. Studies of relatives of people with diabetes showed that those with antibodies against islet cells (ICAs) were far more likely to develop diabetes than relatives whose blood tested negative for the antibodies. Later, researchers discovered antibodies against insulin itself and against one of the pancreatic enzymes (GAD). These antibodies, too, could be used for predictive tests that provide a warning up to seven years before a person at risk actually develops diabetes. "We have proven experience with the predictors and they will only get better," says Dr. Richard Jackson of the Joslin Diabetes Center.[2] Using antibody tests to identify people at risk, researchers are now working on ways of stopping the body from mounting an autoimmune attack on the beta cells—ways to help prevent Type I diabetes from developing.

Preventing Type I Diabetes

At the University of Florida in Gainesville, one patient has been receiving the immunosuppressant drug azathioprine. He was expected to develop diabetes seven years ago, but has not developed the disease. Other immunosuppressants such as

Peggy Polopolus (above) was successfully treated with the new type of drug therapy consisting of immunosuppressant drugs. These drugs suppress the immune system and are used to prevent diabetes from developing in people who are susceptible to the disease.

cyclosporin are also being studied. However, these drugs suppress the entire immune system, so a patient taking them is susceptible to infections. The drugs can also be toxic. So researchers are looking at safer approaches, such as the following.

Vitamin B-3. Vitamin B-3 is inexpensive and safe, and in high doses it protects mice against diabetes. Researchers believe the vitamin helps boost the beta cells' defenses against attack.

Dr. Robert Elliot of the University of Auckland School of Medicine in New Zealand and Dr. Peter Chase of the Barbara Davis Center for Childhood Diabetes in Denver tested vitamin B-3 on children with high ICAs. Only one of fourteen children who received the vitamin developed diabetes, but all eight who were not treated developed the disease. Dr. Elliot has now broadened his studies in New Zealand. Meanwhile, a huge five-year study called the European Nicotinamide Diabetes Intervention Trial (END-IT), combining forces of researchers throughout Europe, began late in 1992.

Beta-cell rest. In the "beta-cell rest" approach a person at high risk for diabetes is given low-dose injections of insulin. Since beta cells produce only as much insulin as the body needs, supplying the hormone from an outside source makes them "shut down." Lymphocytes do not attack the beta cells while they are "resting" in this way. In a pilot study at Joslin Diabetes Center only one out of five patients treated with beta-cell rest developed diabetes, but all seven who refused the therapy developed the disease. Now four centers are beginning a large trial of beta-cell rest in high-risk prediabetics.

Oral insulin. Dr. Howard Weiner and colleagues at Brigham and Women's Hospital in Boston, working with Joslin researchers, have shown that insulin taken by mouth prevents diabetes in a breed of mice that naturally develop the disease. Scientists have discovered that when some proteins are eaten, the body's immune response toward them is changed. This is called oral tolerance. Only a small amount of insulin taken orally reaches the bloodstream, so it has very little effect on blood glucose levels. Researchers at Joslin and the University of Florida College of Medicine are beginning tests on high-risk relatives of patients to see whether diabetes can be prevented, as well as on those who have been newly diagnosed with diabetes to see whether less injected insulin will be required.[3]

Researchers at the University of Florida College of Medicine are trying a similar approach with oral GAD. GAD antibodies are the first sign of an autoimmune response, so if diabetes can be reversed at this stage very little damage to the pancreas will have occurred. Studies on mice have been promising, and the Florida researchers plan to proceed with human tests. Meanwhile, research teams at the University of California at San Francisco and Stanford University have had encouraging results using an injected form of the enzyme. NOD mice (a strain especially bred for a tendency to develop diabetes) were protected from getting the disease by injections

These doctors as the University of Florida are testing a procedure for identifying autoantibodies in people at risk for developing diabetes.

of GAD given when the mice were three weeks old, before the autoimmune attack on the pancreas started.[4]

A research team headed by Dr. Irun Cohen, an immunologist at the Weizmann Institute in Rehovot, Israel, has isolated an antigen that is recognized by the "outlaw" white blood cells that attack beta cells in NOD mice. Injecting this antigen, produced from part of a human protein, into these diabetes-prone mice protected their beta cells from the autoimmune attack. "It's well known in immunology that the same antigen that causes an immune system response can also cause the response to stop," said Dr. Cohen.[5] White blood cells in people who have recently developed Type I diabetes also recognize the antigen. Researchers hope to use it for an early diagnostic test and a vaccine against diabetes.

Retraining the immune system. Researchers at the University of Pennsylvania, led by Dr. Ali Naji, are trying to "retrain" the autoimmune systems in people in the early stages of diabetes. They believe the white blood cells that launch an autoimmune attack on beta cells can be "taught to behave." They hope to do this by injecting islet cells into the thymus gland, where some of the white blood cells mature. A successful experiment on diabetes-prone rats "confirms that we can get very effective prevention of diabetes in this way," says Dr. Naji.[6]

Meanwhile, in Melbourne, Australia, Dr. Len Harrison has made a group of young diabetics less dependent on insulin injections, by using a vaccine made from their own blood. In a technique called photopheresis, white blood cells were removed from the patients' blood and chemically changed to make them seem foreign to the body's immune defenses. Then the treated cells were reinjected. The immune system attacked them, along with the rest of the "outlaw" cells, and there was no further loss of beta cells.[7]

Preventing Type II Diabetes

Obesity. This is one of the biggest risk factors for non-insulin-dependent diabetes. "At least 80 percent of those who get Type II diabetes weigh 20 percent or more than they should and usually have for many years," says John L. Guerigian of

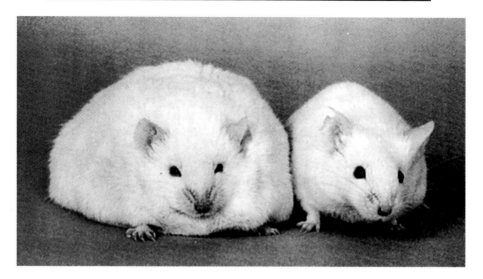

Much recent diabetes research has been done on NOD mice, such as the one on the right, bred for a susceptibility to the disease. The mouse on the left has genes for diabetes and obesity.

the FDA.[8] At the East Carolina University School of Medicine in Greenville, North Carolina, researchers proved that losing weight can prevent non-insulin-dependent diabetes. "These people didn't have to lose all their excess weight to prevent diabetes. Just losing half of the excess body weight was enough to prevent diabetes," says Dr. Jose Caro, the principal investigator in the study.[9]

Dr. Caro believes that people should be screened for impaired glucose tolerance. There are twelve million Americans with IGT and according to Dr. Caro, statistically, up to 9 percent of them develop diabetes each year. With weight loss this number could be greatly reduced.

Eating a more sensible diet is one important factor in controlling weight. Exercise is also extremely important. Studies have shown that exercise can protect against Type II diabetes. "In my opinion, there are actually very few patients with diabetes, Type I or Type II, who should not be exercising," says Dr. Guyton Hornsby, Jr., of the West Virginia School of Physical Education in Morgantown.[10] Even when patients have undergone a doctor-supervised weight-loss program, diet and exercise must continue to play an important role in the patient's daily life.

Chromium. Since the 1950s, studies have suggested that eating foods rich in the trace mineral chromium could help people at risk for Type II diabetes to improve their glucose tolerance, and delay or even prevent the development of the disease. Recently, Dr. Richard Anderson of the Beltsville Human Nutrition Center in Maryland gave 200-microgram chromium supplements to seventeen people with high glucose levels but no diabetes symptoms. After taking the mineral supplements, these prediabetics had blood sugar levels nearly 50 percent lower than when they were on a low-chromium diet. A control group of people with normal glucose levels showed no change.[11] Two servings of broccoli a day would provide enough chromium for a protective effect. In general, wheat bran, fruits, and vegetables are good sources of this mineral. Since these foods are also high in fiber and relatively low in calories, they are also good nutritional choices for controlling weight.

9

Diabetes and the Future

Thirteen-year-old Gary Krajewski, whom we met in earlier chapters, accepts his daily routine of glucose testing and insulin shots, but he doesn't expect to go on that way for the rest of his life. "They're so close to having a cure," he says. "I figure five to six years and I don't have this anymore. I'm bettin' on it."[1]

Today's diabetes researchers are following many different paths toward better treatment and a cure for diabetes. Some are studying the genetics of diabetes to determine how it can best be predicted and prevented. Some researchers are studying the biochemistry behind how insulin is produced and how it functions. Others are studying the complications of the disease that can kill patients with diabetes.

In recent years a lot of advances have made life easier and better for people with diabetes. Many different organizations are contributing.

In 1950 Congress established the National Institute of Diabetes and Kidney Diseases (NIDDK) as one of the National Institutes of Health. Its mission is to improve health through biomedical research.

In recent years researchers at the Joslin Diabetes Center have learned how to predict Type I diabetes, and they are developing methods of prevention; similar advances for Type II diabetes are beginning to emerge.

The Juvenile Diabetes Foundation has provided more than $100 million in funding over the years, in the belief that research will find a cure for diabetes.[2] A special 1993 Research Progress Report edition of their magazine *Countdown* outlines six "Programs of Excellence," promising research programs that the foundation currently supports.[3] In these and other studies, researchers are attempting to find out more about the causes of diabetes and how it develops, and to devise better ways of testing, predicting, treating, and preventing the disease and its complications.

Diabetes Genes?

Doctors have long believed that diabetes is at least partly a hereditary disease. Until recently, however, scientists had not been able to find a gene that caused diabetes. In 1992 a breakthrough was made when a team of French and American researchers reported the discovery of a gene on chromosome 7 that controls the production of glucokinase. This enzyme helps to regulate the secretion of insulin in response to a rise in the blood sugar level. The researchers found a mutation in this gene among fifteen members of a French family with MODY (maturity-onset diabetes of the young), a rare form of Type II diabetes that strikes before the age of twenty-five.[4]

Between 100,000 and 500,000 Americans suffer from MODY. As with most people who have Type II diabetes, most MODY patients do not have to take insulin, but they have an increased risk for such ailments as heart disease, blindness, and kidney failure. Dr. Graeme I. Bell of the University of Chicago, who led the American group, believes that this defective gene could account for 80 percent of MODY cases. Bell's group has also found defective forms of the same gene in a family with the more common form of Type II diabetes, which usually develops later in life as people age or become obese.[5]

This was the first time that a gene has been linked to any type of diabetes. Early in 1993, Finnish researchers from Helsinki University Hospital announced that they had found a mutant form of a different gene in nearly one-third of a group of 107 people with diabetes. This mutant gene, which produces an enzyme that controls the storage of sugar in the form of glycogen, was present in only 8 percent of 164 nondiabetics.[6]

Diabetes researchers are excited. Now that genes linked with Type II diabetes have been found, they can begin working on ways to cure patients by "fixing" faulty genes through gene therapy. Many doctors and researchers, as well as people with diabetes are hopeful that genetic cures will be available in the not too distant future.

Looking for an Insulin Switch

People with Type I diabetes produce little or no insulin, but those with non-insulin-dependent diabetes often produce plenty. Why isn't their insulin effective at regulating blood sugar levels? Marc d'Alarcao at Tufts University believes that the problem is in the target cells in the fat, liver, and kidneys. Normally, when insulin is present, target cells release a chemical that allows the cell to consume sugar molecules. The Tufts research group is trying to synthesize a portion of this chemical to create a turn-on "switch" that can "nudge" target cells into using sugar properly. Dr. d'Alarcao believes that other cellular switches may eventually be devised that would, for example, activate immune cells against cancer cells.[7]

"Ouchless" Glucose Monitoring

When Robert D. Rosenthal, the president of Futrex Inc., received a letter from a concerned grandmother of a girl with diabetes, he felt compelled to accept the challenge to invent a way to measure blood glucose without drawing blood. The grandmother had seen a story about Futrex's no-pain device for measuring body fat, and she was hoping the company could develop a similar device to measure glucose levels, to free her granddaughter from the painful blood-testing routine. Now dozens of companies are working to become the first to create a "Dream Beam."[8]

In experimental prototypes, a finger is placed inside the monitor, and near-infrared light shines through the skin tissue. Faint signals are emitted when glucose absorbs specific wavelengths of light. Those signals must be deciphered against the background noise made by the signals from other tissue and blood components. A miniature computer analyzes the wavelengths absorbed by glucose and determines the blood glucose concentration. The meter can provide continuous glucose measurements, yielding information about fluctuations in glucose concentrations. None of the devices have yet received approval from the FDA, but given the keen competition to be the first to come out with an "ouchless" monitoring device, it is expected that one will be available within the next few years.[9]

Chemist George Wilson at the University of Kansas is trying to create tiny implantable electrodes that would constantly measure blood glucose levels and set off an alarm whenever they got too high.[10] Ultimately, researchers hope to combine an "ouchless" glucose monitor with a programmable insulin pump. The exact amount of insulin needed would be automatically delivered, based on glucose levels. This would essentially replace nonworking beta cells, eliminating the need for insulin injections, and it would be a more perfect insulin delivery system.

Better Treatment Methods

Nasal insulin. Many people with diabetes would like to see insulin available in an easier-to-take form. A number of drugs are available as nasal sprays, for example, and work quickly and effectively. However, doctors usually advise against long-term use of nasal sprays because the membranes in the nasal passages are very delicate. Nasal delivery of insulin presents some additional difficulties. The insulin molecule is too large to be absorbed across the nasal membrane. Researchers are trying to get around this problem by adding ingredients that help the body absorb insulin. After extensive tests in diabetic dogs and a small clinical trial on humans, researchers at Temple University in Philadelphia believe that licorice might be the perfect delivery vehicle. Larger clinical trials will be conducted to find out for sure.[11]

Meanwhile, at the Johns Hopkins School of Public Health, researchers are working on an aerosol inhaler that delivers insulin vapors to the lungs. There they are absorbed into the blood through the thin membranes of the alveoli, the tiny air sacs from which oxygen is absorbed from the air we breathe.[12]

Oral insulin. Insulin is a protein, and proteins are broken down by the acid in the stomach. So attempts to develop a pill form of insulin, which could be swallowed, seemed doomed to failure. But researchers at Hadassah-Hebrew University Medical Center in Jerusalem have produced an experimental capsule with a coating that protects the contents from stomach acid, then releases them in the small intestine. The capsule contains insulin together with bile salts, which help the hormone to be absorbed through the intestinal wall, and a soybean derivative that protects the hormone from being digested by the intestinal juices. According to Dr. Hanoch Bar-On, head of the center's Diabetic Unit, the oral insulin is good only for Type II diabetes. Not enough is absorbed to be effective for Type I diabetes.[13]

Insulinotropin. A hormone discovered in 1986 at Massachusetts General Hospital may provide a more natural way of regulating blood sugar level for people with Type II diabetes. Insulinotropin is produced in the intestines when we eat and stimulates the pancreas to release insulin. In animal studies and human tests, continuous intravenous infusions of insulinotropin caused the blood insulin levels to triple when glucose flooded into the blood after a meal; but then the insulin levels fell as the blood sugar levels dropped. There were no hypoglycemic insulin reactions, said Dr. Joel F. Habener, head of the Massachusetts research team, even with "whopping doses" of insulinotropin.[14] Researchers believe that wide swings in glucose levels are responsible for many complications of diabetes, such as blindness, arteriosclerosis, and kidney damage. If insulinotropin could provide a smoother response of insulin to rising blood sugar levels, it might also aid in preventing complications.

Better Prevention of Complications

Diabetes is still the leading cause of blindness for those under sixty-five. Laser surgery has been able to slow the damage. But researcher Theodore Hollis at the Pennsylvania State University and ophthalmologist Thomas Gardner believe they have discovered how diabetes causes blindness. They found that histamines (the body chemicals involved in allergic reactions, such as the runny nose in hay fever and the swelling in hives) were causing blood vessels to leak, leading them to think the long-term effects of leaking blood vessels and histamines might be the cause of blindness. The researchers have shown that antihistamines (the drugs used to treat allergies) prevent blood vessel leaks and eye damage in rats. Clinical trials in humans look promising, too.[15]

Another approach to preventing blindness and nerve destruction is focused on the role of the sugar sorbitol. A key enzyme in the reactions that change glucose into sorbitol is aldose reductase. Various drugs that stop the enzyme's action have shown some promise for preventing diabetic complications. Studies of some of these drugs are under way, and one of them, tolrestat, is available in Europe.[16]

A three-year study conducted on more than 400 patients with Type I diabetes at thirty medical centers in the United States and Canada revealed that captopril, a drug used to treat high blood pressure, can prevent or greatly delay the development of kidney failure. According to Dr. James R. Gavin 3d, president of the American Diabetes Association, about half of people with Type I diabetes eventually develop severe kidney damage. Then they need kidney dialysis (at a cost of more than $44,000 a year for each patient) or a kidney transplant to stay alive. Researchers had found that diabetes increases the pressure in the walls of the tiny blood vessels that filter blood in the kidneys and eventually damages them. Captopril helps to prevent this harmful pressure rise. Dr. Gavin called the study one of the most important discoveries in diabetes research in a quarter century.[17] A new study is now under way to determine whether captropril can also prevent severe kidney damage in people with Type II diabetes.

Transplanting Insulin-Producing Cells

Kidneys, hearts, lungs, and livers have been successfully transplanted to save the lives of people whose own organs had failed. Naturally, diabetes researchers thought of pancreas transplants as a possible "cure" for diabetes. The first pancreas transplant was performed in 1966. It was not successful. Eventually, more effective techniques were worked out, but transplanting a whole pancreas is a very complicated operation. (Remember, the pancreas produces strong digestive enzymes in addition to its hormones.) Moreover, transplant patients must receive powerful immunosuppressive drugs to prevent the body from attacking the transplanted organ. These drugs have side effects, and may leave the patients unable to fight off infections and cancer.

Some researchers turned to the idea of transplanting only the beta cells, rather than the whole pancreas. Human patients have already received transplanted beta cells. But this kind of transplant, too, requires immunosuppressants to keep the body from rejecting the transplants. In addition, there are not enough human islet cells available for transplantation. Only one thousand human pancreases are available in the United States each year, and two or three of them are needed to provide the islet cells for a single transplant recipient.

Several different research groups are trying to find ways around these problems. Researchers at the Diabetes Research Center at Albert Einstein College of Medicine in the Bronx, New York, aim to genetically alter the islet cells so that the body will not reject them. "The surface of transplanted cells will be altered using two different molecular biology approaches so that the normal immune system of a diabetes patient no longer recognizes them as foreign invaders," explains Dr. Michael Brownlee. "To provide sufficient numbers of the genetically engineered cells, we plan to turn beta cell growth on in the laboratory in a reversible way, grow an adequate number of cells, and then turn growth off again before transplantation. Normally, insulin-producing cells do not multiply, whether inside the body or in a laboratory dish."[18] If the Brownlee group succeeds, transplanting insulin-producing cells could be a safe procedure, and a cure for Type I diabetes.

At the Stanford University School of Medicine researchers are trying to find a way to suppress only the white blood cells involved in the attack on beta cells, not the entire immune system. One question they are seeking to answer is whether the attack is caused by a defect in the immune system or is due to a change in a beta-cell surface protein. Another experiment at Stanford will involve replacing the immune systems of diabetic mice with special cells called "stem cells" from healthy nondiabetic mice. These stem cells mature into immune system cells, which the researchers hope will prevent the immune system from attacking beta cells.

In experiments the at University of Pennsylvania, when islet cells were transplanted into the thymus glands of diabetic rats, the rats' bodies lost their ability to reject the new islet cells, even if they were later transplanted to other parts of the body. Meanwhile, the transplanted cells produced insulin when it was needed and cured the rats' diabetes.[19]

In 1991 researchers at Washington University School of Medicine in St. Louis, Missouri, working with CytoTherapeutics Inc. of Providence, Rhode Island, took insulin-producing islet cells from the pancreases of rats and mixed them into a gel. The gel was placed inside tiny plastic fibers, each about an inch long and as thick as a paper clip. The fibers were implanted under the skin of diabetic mice. The cells released insulin when blood sugar levels went up, and there were no signs of rejection. The reason was that the fibers were somewhat permeable, permitting glucose molecules to enter the fibers and insulin molecules to pass out; but their pores were too small for immune-system cells to enter and destroy the islet cells. The blood sugar levels in the mice were near normal within a week, and 80 percent of the mice had normal blood sugar levels for at least two months afterward. Using a similar procedure with islet cells from dogs, cows, and pigs, researchers at BioHybrid Technologies Inc. in Shrewsbury, Massachusetts, were also able to control blood sugar levels in diabetic rats[20] and developed an "artificial pancreas" in which blood is routed through porous tubes surrounded by pancreas cells.[21]

In 1994 Dr. Patrick Soon-Shiong of St. Vincent's Medical Center in Los Angeles announced that a patient with Type I diabetes had been able to stop taking insulin injections after receiving two doses of encapsulated islet cells. In a technique developed by his research group, human beta cells were enclosed in microscopic gel capsules made from seaweed extract and injected into the patient's abdominal cavity. The transplanted cells responded to rises in the blood sugar level by secreting insulin, which was taken up by blood vessels leading to the liver. Eight months after the transplant, moreover, tests showed that diabetic nerve damage had been reversed.

Promising as these new transplant techniques are, there is still the problem of supply. Far too few human pancreases are available to supply the needs of all the people with Type I diabetes; and several animals would be needed to supply enough beta cells for one human recipient. The process of extracting the cells from the pancreas is complicated and expensive, too.

At Dalhousie University in Halifax, Nova Scotia, Dr. James R. Wright, Jr. is working on isolating insulin-producing islet tissue from fish. In some fish the islet cells are found not in the pancreas but in separate structures called Brockmann bodies. They are much easier to isolate, says Dr. Wright: "You simply cut open the fish's abdomen, cut away the membrane between the stomach and the liver, and there they are."[22] He estimates that the job of isolating islet cells from pancreases accounts for 90 to 95 percent of the cost of islet transplantation research, so the use of fish would bring a huge saving. He is working with tilapia, an African fish species that is raised as a food fish on fish farms in various parts of the world. Experiments on diabetic mice have shown that transplanted tilapia islets can produce insulin and successfully regulate the blood sugar level.

In 1992 scientists at the University of Texas Southwest Medical Center announced that they had produced a new source of insulin-secreting cells that could be used in an "artificial pancreas." They started with a line of cells from the mouse pituitary gland, which can be grown in test tubes. A team at the University of California, San Francisco, had genetically engineered these cells to produce insulin. (Normally, pituitary cells produce other hormones.) At first the altered mouse cells did not turn their insulin production on and off in response to blood glucose levels. The Texas researchers discovered that the cells were lacking a key gene that would allow glucose from the blood to enter. When the missing gene was inserted, the cells acted very much like pancreatic beta cells. Dr. Christopher Newgard, the leader of the team, said that the new cells needed some more tinkering—they began producing insulin a bit too soon, and they also produced a mouse hormone, ACTH, which might cause side effects. But he expected that within three to five years they would be ready for tests in humans.[23]

Treatments from Unexpected Places

Traditionally, most scientists have downplayed folk medicine cure-alls made of herbs or mineral compounds. However, some researchers are excited about vanadium, a natural mineral found in the soil, all plants and animals, and most of the foods we eat. Claims of blood-sugar-lowering effects dating back to 1899 have recently been supported by animal studies. Some vanadium compounds lower blood sugar levels and increase sensitivity to insulin. Researchers believe, though, that at least some insulin may be necessary for vanadium compounds to work effectively. Researchers warn that human tests need to proceed with caution. "Vanadium causes a wide range of biological effects, including potentially toxic ones," points out Dr. Paul Stankeiwicz of Simon Fraser University in British Columbia.[24] If human trials at the Joslin Diabetes Center in Boston and other research centers around the world prove out, vanadium compounds could become a major treatment for people with Type II diabetes, and could help people with Type I diabetes to reduce insulin requirements and keep their blood sugar levels more stable.

A Promising Future

Technological and medical advances have helped make life better for many people with diabetes. Better awareness of methods of prevention has also helped many who are at high risk for diabetes to avoid developing the disease. In the years to come, many more advances will be made that will make it still easier for people with diabetes to lead healthy, normal lives. And there is hope that those with diabetes today may live to see their disease completely cured.

Q&A

Q. What is the pancreas?

A. It is two organs in one: a digestive gland that produces powerful digestive juices that act in the intestine, and an endocrine gland that produces several hormones that help to control the body's storage and use of sugar.

Q. What is insulin?

A. It is a hormone, produced by the beta cells of the pancreas. It helps to lower the blood sugar level by aiding the passage of glucose out of the blood vessels into body cells and helping to convert it to glycogen.

Q. What is the difference between glycogen and glucagon?

A. Glycogen, sometimes called "animal starch," consists of many molecules of the simple sugar glucose, chemically joined together. Glucagon is a hormone, produced by the alpha cells of the pancreas. It helps glycogen to be converted to glucose, which passes into the bloodstream.

Q. Is it bad to have sugar in your blood?

A. No. The simple sugar glucose is the body's main energy fuel. It is produced in the digestion of foods and carried by the blood to cells all over the body. If your blood sugar level is too low, you may feel tired or faint. But too high a blood sugar level can also produce serious problems.

Q. What are the symptoms of diabetes?

A. The symptoms include frequent urination, extreme thirst, hunger, fatigue, irritability, and weight loss. In Type II diabetes symptoms may also include frequent infections, slow healing, blurred vision, and tingling or numbness in the hands or feet.

Q. Can I catch diabetes from someone who has it?

A. You can't catch diabetes by spending time with people who have it, touching them, or sharing food with them. There are no "diabetes germs."

Q. What is the difference between Type I and Type II diabetes?

A. Type I is believed to be due to an autoimmune reaction in which the body attacks its own beta cells until the pancreas can no longer produce enough insulin. It usually (but not always) appears in young people. Type II usually develops in older people and in the obese. The pancreas still produces insulin, but it cannot work effectively.

Q. Do insulin shots cure diabetes?

A. Diabetes can be controlled by insulin shots or other treatments, but they are not cures. The condition still exists, and treatment must be continued throughout the person's life.

Q. What should I do if my friend with diabetes collapses and I'm not sure whether it is an insulin reaction or a diabetic coma?

A. If the friend is conscious, give fruit juice, candy, or some other form of sugar. If he or she is unconscious or does not recover quickly, call a doctor or an emergency number. Insulin reactions develop quickly and are very dangerous. Diabetic coma develops more slowly, so if you made a mistake there will be time to correct it.

Diabetes Timeline

1500 B.C.—Ebers papyrus of ancient Egypt mentioned treatment for diabetes.

400 B.C.—Ancient Indian doctor Susruta wrote about diabetes.

A.D. **100**—Ancient Greek physician Aretaeus of Cappadocia gave diabetes its name.

1600s—English physician Thomas Syndenham found a meat diet improved diabetes.

1683—Swiss doctor Johann Conrad Brunner removed dog's pancreas, but did not realize he had created a model of diabetes.

1766—English physician Matthew Dobson proved sugar was present in diabetic's urine, and that sugar is present in blood of both healthy and diabetic subjects.

1783—English physician Thomas Cawley was first to diagnose diabetes based on sugar in urine.

1864—Norwegian scientist reported patient developed diabetes after mumps.

1869—German medical student Paul Langerhans discovered islets of Langerhans in pancreas.

1899—Joseph von Mering and Oskar Minkowski created dog model of diabetes.

1921—Frederick Banting and Charles Best isolated insulin.

1948—French researchers developed oral hypoglycemic drugs.

1955—Frederick Sanger worked out structure of insulin molecule.

1978—Researchers used genetic technology to synthesize rat insulin.

1983—Genetically produced human insulin made available for diabetics.

1992—First gene involved with diabetes found.

For More Information

American Diabetes Association
1660 Duke Street
Alexandria, VA 22314
(also has state and local chapters)

American Dietetic Association
430 North Michigan Avenue
Chicago, IL 60606
(800) 366-1655

Canadian Diabetes Association
15 Toronto Street, Suite 1001
Toronto, Ontario, Canada
MSC 2E3
(publishes *Diabetes Dialogue* magazine)

Joslin Diabetes Center
One Joslin Place
Boston, MA 02215
(also has affiliated local centers)
(publishes *Joslin Magazine*)

Juvenile Diabetes Research Foundation International
4332 Park Avenue South
New York, NY 10016
(800) 223-1138
(publishes *Countdown* magazine)

National Diabetes Information Clearinghouse
Box NDIC
Bethesda, MD 20892

National Institute of Diabetes and Digestive and Kidney Diseases
National Institutes of Health
Building 31, Room 9A04
Bethesda, MD 10892

Chapter Notes

Chapter 1

1. Dionne Farris, interview, January 31, 1993.

2. Leo P. Krall and Richard S. Beaser, *Joslin Diabetes Manual*, 12th ed., Philadelphia: Lea & Febiger, 1989, p. 1.

3. *Diabetes: 1991 Vital Statistics*, Alexandria, Va.: American Diabetes Association, 1991, p. 1.

4. NDIC Clearinghouse, *Diabetes Overview* (pamphlet), National Institutes of Health, 1992, p. 2.

Chapter 2

1. Alvin Silverstein and Virginia B. Silverstein, *The Sugar Disease: Diabetes*, New York: Lippincott, 1980, p. 46.

2. *Diabetes A to Z*, McLean, Va.: American Diabetes Association, Inc., 1992, p. 42.

Chapter 3

1. Paul Franklin, "Living with Diabetes," *The Courier News* (Bridgewater, N.J.), November 22, 1991, p. B-6.

2. Associated Press, "Study Says Intense Therapy Slows Diabetes Complications," *The Star-Ledger* (Newark, N.J.), June 14, 1993, p. 1.

Chapter 4

1. Clare Collins, "Diabolical Diabetes," *American Health*, January–February 1993, p. 70.

2. Judith Randal, "Insulin Key to Diabetes but Not Full Cure," *FDA Consumer*, May 1992, p. 17.

Chapter 5

1. Harvey J. Fields, "A Whole New Ball Game," *The New York Times Magazine*, April 1, 1990, p. 20.

2. *Diabetes: 1991 Vital Statistics*, Alexandria, Va.: American Diabetes Association, 1991, p. 23.

3. "Cow's Milk & Molecular Mimicry," *Countdown*, Winter 1993, p. 16.

4. Ibid., p. 18.

Chapter 6

1. Leo P. Krall and Richard S. Beaser, *Joslin Diabetes Manual*, 12th ed. Philadelphia: Lea & Febiger, 1989, p. 155.

2. Judith Randal, "Insulin Key to Diabetes but Not Full Cure," *FDA Consumer*, May 1992, p. 18.

3. Paul Franklin, "Living with Diabetes," *The Courier News* (Bridgewater, N.J.), November 22, 1991, p. B-6.

4. Clare Collins, "Diabolical Diabetes," *American Health*, January–February 1993, p. 71.

5. Sandra Blakeslee, "Doctors Announce Way to Forestall Effect of Diabetes," *The New York Times*, June 14, 1993, p. A1.

6. Michael Waldholz, "Intense Regime Found to Check Diabetes Effects," *The Wall Street Journal*, June 14, 1993, p. B6D.

7. Richard Agrin, "A New Plan in the Offing for Diabetes," *The Courier News* (Bridgewater, N.J.), June 2, 1993, p. D-1.

8. "'Smarter' Insulin Pumps on the Horizon," *Countdown*, Winter 1993, p. 34.

9. Krall and Beaser, p. 35.

10. Ibid., p. 39.

11. Ibid.

Chapter 7

1. Elisabeth Rosenthal, "Life on the Edge," *Discover*, March 1991, p. 76.

2. Clare Collins, "Diabolical Diabetes," *American Health*, January–February 1993, p. 72.

3. Bret Michaels, "Rocky Road," *People Weekly*, August 23, 1993, pp. 63, 64.

4. *Periodontal Disease and Diabetes: A Guide for Patients*, NIH Publication No. 87-2046 (pamphlet), September 1987, p. 3.

5. Rosenthal, p. 78.

6. "Tough Times Get Tougher," Joslin Diabetes Center pamphlet, p. 1.

7. Ibid.

Chapter 8

1. Robert S. Dinsmoor, "Better Prediction Spurs New Approaches to Prevention," *Countdown*, Winter 1993, p. 6.

2. Ibid., p. 8.

3. Ibid., p. 13.

4. Associated Press, "Researchers Block Form of Diabetes in Mice," *The New York Times*, November 4, 1993, p. A15.

5. "Can a Vaccine Stop Diabetes?" *Countdown*, Fall 1991, p. 22.

6. Associated Press, "Rogue Cells in Diabetes Are Tamed, Study Says," *The New York Times*, May 30, 1992, p. 7.

7. Ian Anderson, "Self-Vaccination Halts March of Diabetes," *New Scientist*, August 10, 1991, p. 19.

8. Judith Randal, "Insulin Key to Diabetes but Not Full Cure," *FDA Consumer*, May 1992, p. 17.

9. Andrew Keegan, et al., "Bringing Research to Light," *Diabetes Forecast*, September 1992, p. 36.

10. Ibid., p. 41.

11. "Eating Broccoli Helps Fight Type II Diabetes," *Insight*, February 4, 1991, p. 57.

Chapter 9

1. Paul Franklin, "Patients Learn to Cope with Disease," *The Courier News* (Bridgewater, N.J.), November 22, 1991, p. B-6.

2. JDF letter, 1992.

3. Sandy Dylak, "The Programs of Excellence," *Countdown*, Winter 1993, pp. 19–31.

4. Associated Press, "Abnormal Gene Linked to Some Cases of Diabetes," *The New York Times*, May 3, 1992, p. 36L; "Diabetes," *The World* Book Health & Medical Annual 1993, Chicago: World Book, 1993, p. 311.

5. "Gene Flaw Found in Uncommon Diabetes," *Science News*, May 2, 1992, p. 300.

6. Associated Press, "Gene Linked to Diabetes Is Found," *The New York Times*, January 12, 1993, p. C3.

7. "Looking for the Insulin Switch," *Pharmacy Times*, November 1992, p. 22.

8. Ivan Amato, "Race Quickens for Non-Stick Blood Monitoring Technology," *Science*, November 6, 1992, p. 892.

9. "Taking the 'Ouch' Out of Blood Glucose Monitoring," *Countdown*, Winter 1993, p. 33.

10. Amato, p. 893.

11. "Nasal Insulin—Will the Final Formula Smell Like Licorice?" *Countdown*, Winter 1993, pp. 32–33.

12. "No More Shots for People with Diabetes?" *Current Science*, September 3, 1993, p. 13.

13. "Insulin Tablet Effective in Late-Onset Diabetic Cases," *Medical Tribune*, July 11, 1991, p. 15.

14. David Stipp, "Diabetes Drug is Shown to Outperform Insulin Shots in Regulating Blood Sugar," *The Wall Street Journal*, January 20, 1992, p. B6.

15. "A Common Drug May Fight Blindness in Diabetics," *Business Week*, February 7, 1992, p. 129.

16. Colman Cassidy, "Drug for Diabetics Goes on Sale in Ireland," *New Scientist*, July 15, 1989, p. 35; Carole Bullock, "'Sorbinil Is Dead' But ARIs Are Not," *Medical Tribune*, September 28, 1989, p. 6.

17. Gina Kolata, "Drug Found to Stall Failure of Kidneys in Some Diabetics," *The New York Times*, November 11, 1993, p. A1.

18. Sandy Dylak, "The Programs of Excellence," *Countdown*, Winter 1993, p. 23.

19. Gina Kolata, "Rat Immune System Is Taught to Accept Transplant, Researchers Say," *The New York Times*, September 14, 1990, p. A18.

20. "Diabetes," *The World Book Health & Medical Annual 1993*, Chicago: World Book, 1993, p. 310.

21. "On the Horizon for Diabetics: an Artificial Pancreas," *U.S. News & World Report*, May 4, 1992, p. 99.

22. Wayne L. Clark, "Fishing for a Cure," *Countdown*, Fall 1993, p. 13.

23. Jerry E. Bishop, "Cell Advance Holds Promise for Diabetes," *The Wall Street Journal*, January 15, 1992, p. B1.

24. "Ancient Myths & Common Minerals," *Countdown*, Winter 1993, p. 37.

Glossary

alpha cells—Pancreatic cells that produce the hormone glucagon.

antibody—A protein produced by the immune system to attack a foreign chemical (antigen); part of the body's defenses against disease germs.

antigen—A protein or other chemical that is recognized as "foreign" by the immune system and provokes the production of antibodies.

autoimmune disease—A disorder resulting from a mistaken attack by the immune system against the body's own tissues.

beta-cell rest—An experimental approach to prevention of Type I diabetes by giving low doses of insulin to prevent autoimmune destruction of beta cells.

beta cells—Pancreatic cells that produce the hormone insulin.

blood sugar level—The amount of glucose in the circulating blood.

blood glucose monitors—Devices that determine the blood sugar level.

chronic disease—One that persists for a long time.

diabetes insipidus—A rare type of diabetes in which large amounts of urine are produced, but it does not contain sugar.

diabetes mellitus—A condition in which insulin is not produced or does not properly regulate the body's use and storage of sugar, resulting in the presence of abnormally high amounts of glucose in the blood; excess glucose may also spill over into the urine.

diabetic—Pertaining to diabetes. (Many health professionals now prefer not to use "diabetic" as a noun to denote people with diabetes.)

diabetic coma—See ketoacidosis.

diabetic retinitis—A serious eye disorder resulting from rupture of tiny blood vessels in the retina, the light-sensitive layer at the back of the eyeball.

endocrine glands—Body structures that produce hormones and secrete them into the bloodstream, which carries them to their site of action.

exchanges—Substitutions of foods with equivalent nutrient content.

exocrine glands—Body structures that produce digestive enzymes or other substances that are secreted into ducts leading directly to their site of action.

fasting blood glucose level—The concentration of glucose in the blood after a long period without eating.

GAD—Glutamic acid decarboxylase, an enzyme produced by the beta cells of the pancreas; antibodies to GAD are the basis of a diagnostic test.

gestational diabetes—A type of diabetes that appears in some women during pregnancy, then disappears after the baby is born.

glucagon—A hormone produced in the pancreas that stimulates the conversion of stored glycogen to glucose and the release of glucose into the bloodstream; its action results in raising the blood sugar level.

glucokinase—An enzyme that helps to regulate insulin secretion.

glucose—A simple sugar; the main fuel substance for body cells.

glucose tolerance test—A diagnostic test in which the blood sugar level is measured before and at intervals after drinking a glucose solution.

glucosuria—The presence of glucose in the urine.

glycogen—"Animal starch," a starch formed by linking many glucose molecules together, providing for compact storage in animal tissues.

hormone—A chemical messenger that travels through the bloodstream and helps to control and coordinate body processes.

hyperglycemia—A higher-than-normal blood sugar level.

hypoglycemia—A lower-than-normal blood sugar level.

ICAs—Islet-cell antibodies, present in people with established or developing Type I diabetes.

IDDM—Insulin-dependent diabetes mellitus: persistent hyperglycemia in which little or no insulin is produced; usually develops in children or young adults; also called Type I diabetes; formerly called juvenile diabetes.

immunosuppressant—A drug that blocks antibody formation or other immune system reactions.

impaired glucose tolerance—Higher-than-normal blood glucose levels, but not high enough to be classified as diabetes.

insulin—A hormone produced in the pancreas that stimulates the passage of glucose from the blood into body cells and promotes the conversion of glucose to storage forms such as glycogen and fatty acids; its action results in a lowering of the blood sugar level.

insulin reaction—Hypoglycemia resulting from taking too much insulin (or failing to eat the expected amount of food after taking insulin).

insulin resistance—A condition in which insulin cannot enter cells because there are insufficient or impaired receptors on the cell surface.

insulin pump—A device (either worn or surgically implanted) that delivers insulin continuously.

insulinase—An enzyme that breaks down insulin after it has done its job.

insulinotropin—An intestinal hormone that stimulates insulin secretion.

islets of Langerhans—Clusters of insulin-producing cells scattered through the pancreas.

ketoacidosis—A buildup of toxic ketone bodies in the blood that occurs when the body is using fats instead of sugars as energy fuel.

ketone bodies—Somewhat acidic chemicals produced as by-products when fats are used for energy; they have a fruity, "acetone" odor.

Lente insulin—A modified form of insulin with an intermediate time of action.

MODY—Maturity-onset diabetes of the young: a rare form of Type II diabetes that develops before the age of twenty-five.

molecular mimicry—an accidental similarity of environmental chemicals to normal body chemicals.

NIDDM—Non-insulin-dependent diabetes mellitus: persistent hyperglycemia in which body cells do not respond properly to insulin; usually appears in middle age or later; also called Type II diabetes; formerly called adult-onset diabetes.

oral hypoglycemic drugs—Drugs taken by mouth that help to regulate the blood sugar level; used in Type II diabetes.

predisposition—A hereditary tendency to develop a disease (such as diabetes) if suitable environmental conditions exist.

receptors—Specific chemicals on the cell surface that react with hormones or other "messenger substances."

recombinant insulin—Synthetic human insulin produced by inserting insulin-producing genes into bacteria.

somatostatin—A hormone secreted by the pancreas that helps to regulate insulin and glucagon secretion.

sulfonlureas—A chemical class including some oral hypoglycemic drugs.

Type I diabetes—Alternative name for insulin-dependent diabetes mellitus (IDDM).

Type II diabetes—Alternative name for non-insulin-dependent diabetes mellitus (NIDDM).

Ultralente insulin—A slow-acting modified form of insulin.

Further Reading

Books

Anderson, Barbara J., Mary T. Burkhart, and Denise Charron-Prochownik. *Making Choices: Teenagers and Diabetes*. Ann Arbor: University of Michigan, 1986.

Biermann, June, and Barbara Toohey. *The Diabetic's Book*. Los Angeles: Jeremy Tarcher, 1990.

Diabetes A to Z. Alexandria, Va.: American Diabetes Association, 1992.

Goodheart. Barbara. Diabetes. New York: Franklin Watts, 1990.

Herman, William H., ed. Take Charge of Your Diabetes: A Guide for Patients. Washington, D.C.: U.S. Department of Health & Human Services, Public Health Service, 1991.

Krall, Leo P., and Richard Beaser. *Joslin Diabetes Manual*. 12th ed. Philadelphia: Lea & Febiger, 1989.

Moy, Claudia Scala, ed. *Diabetes: 1991 Vital Statistics*. Alexandria, Va.: American Diabetes Association, 1991.

National Diabetes Information Clearinghouse. The Diabetes Dictionary. Washington, D.C.: U.S. Department of Health and Human Services, Public Health Service, 1989 (NIH Pub. No. 89-3016). (Also available in Spanish: *Diccionario de la Diabetes*. Pub. No. 91-3016S de los NIH.)

Taylor, Barbara. *Living with Diabetes*. New York: Franklin Watts, 1989.

Tiger, Steven. *Understanding Disease: Diabetes*. New York: Julian Messner, 1987.

Pamphlets

About Joslin Diabetes Center. Joslin Diabetes Center.

Diabetes in Adults. U.S. Department of Health and Human Services, Public Health Service, 1990 (NIH Pub. No. 90-2904).

Diabetes Overview. NDIC Clearinghouse, National Institute of Diabetes and Digestive and Kidney Diseases, 1992 (NIH Pub. No. 92-3235).

Diabetes Special Report. National Institute of Diabetes and Digestive and Kidney Diseases, 1992 (NIH Pub. No. 92-3422).

Helping Research Find a Cure. Juvenile Diabetes Foundation International, No. 2.

Insulin-Dependent Diabetes. U.S. Department of Health and Human Services, Public Health Service, 1990 (NIH Pub. No. 90-2098).

JDF and You: The Search for a Cure. Juvenile Diabetes Foundation International, No. 1.

Just Like Any Other Kid. Canadian Diabetes Association, 1991.

Monitoring Your Blood Sugar. Juvenile Diabetes Foundation International, No. 7.

Periodontal Disease and Diabetes: A Guide for Parents. U.S. Department of Health and Human Services, Public Health Service, 1987 (NIH Pub. No. 87-2946).

25 Facts About Diabetes. Joslin Diabetes Center.

Your Child Has Diabetes. Juvenile Diabetes Foundation International, No. 5.

Articles

Amato, Ivan. "Race Quickens for Non-Stick Blood Monitoring Technology." *Science,* November 6, 1992, pp. 892–893.

"Ancient Myths and Common Minerals." *Countdown,* Winter 1993, pp. 36–37.

Associated Press. "Abnormal Gene Linked to Some Cases of Diabetes." *The New York Times,* May 3, 1992, p. 36.

Associated Press. "Rogue Cells in Diabetes Are Tamed, Study Says." *The New York Times,* May 30, 1992, p. 7.

Blakeslee, Sandra. "Doctors Announce Way to Forestall Effect of Diabetes." *The New York Times,* June 14, 1993, pp. A1, A12.

Carey, Benedick. "Dodging Diabetes." *In Health,* January–February 1991, p. 18.

Clark, Wayne L. "Fishing for a Cure." *Countdown,* Fall 1993, pp. 8–16.

Collins, Clare. "Diabolical Diabetes." *American Health,* January–February 1993, pp. 68–72.

Cowen, Ron. "Seeds of Protection." *Science News,* June 2, 1990, pp. 350–351.

"Cow's Milk & Molecular Mimicry." *Countdown,* Winter 1993, pp. 14–18.

Dinsmoor, Robert S. "Better Prediction Spurs New Approaches to Prevention." *Countdown,* Winter 1993, pp. 6–13.

Dylak, Sandy. "The Programs of Excellence: Six of the Boldest Research Projects Ever Established to Find a Cure for Diabetes and Its Complications." *Countdown,* Winter 1993, pp. 19–29.

Fields, Harvey J. "A Whole New Ball Game." *The New York Times Magazine,* April 1, 1990, pp. 20–22.

Grossman, Lorne D. "Food Substitutes and Diabetes: Do They Mix?" *Diabetes Dialogue,* Spring 1993, pp. 28–29.

"Group Strives to Alert People at Risk for Diabetes." *The Star-Ledger* (Newark, N.J.), March 22, 1992, pp. H-1-2.

Keegan, Andrew, et al., "Bringing Research to Light." *Diabetes Forecast,* September 1992, pp. 35–43.

119

Landers, Ann. "Simple Test Tells the Score on Diabetes Risk," *The Star-Ledger* (Newark, N.J.), March 20, 1990.

Levine, S. Robert. "Exercising to Prevent Diabetes." *Countdown*, Winter 1992, pp. 26–27.

"Living Through the Complications of Diabetes." *Joslin Magazine*, Fall 1991, pp. 4–5.

McCullough, Tom. "At Risk for Type II Diabetes? Exercise May Prevent It." *Joslin Magazine*, Fall 1992, pp. 7–8.

McNeill, John H. "Vanadium: A New Insulin?" *Diabetes Dialogue*, Winter 1992, pp. 32–34.

Michaels, Bret. "Rocky Road." *People Weekly*, August 23, 1993, pp. 63–66.

Monsaert, Ronald P. "Diabetes in the Young and the Old: Challenges and Solutions." *Pharmacy Times*, October 1988, pp. 34–38.

Newman, Donna La May. "Diabetes: A Lifetime of Balance." *Vim and Vigor*, Spring 1992, pp. 45–49.

Peters, Barbara McGarry. "Diet and Exercise Regimen Important in Controlling Diabetes." *The Star-Ledger* (Newark, N.J.), January 12, 1992, p. 16.

Randall, Judith. "Insulin Key to Diabetes but Not Full Cure." *FDA Consumer*, May 1992, pp. 15–19.

Rosenthal, Elisabeth. "Life on the Edge." *Discover*, March 1991, pp. 76–78.

Rubin, Rita. "A Tighter Rein on Diabetes." *U.S. News & World Report*, June 28, 1993, p. 68.

Ryan, Margaret. "Why Work Out?" *Countdown*, Winter 1992, pp. 6–13.

Squires, Sally. "Why Us? Blacks and Diabetes." *American Visions*, December 1988, pp. 23–25.

Ubell, Earl. "A Cure for Diabetes?" *Parade Magazine*, April 21, 1985, pp. 12–14.

Waldholz, Michael. "Intense Regime Found to Check Diabetes Effects." *The Wall Street Journal*, June 14, 1993, p. B6D.

Whitlow, Joan. "Double Jeopardy for Diabetes." *The Star-Ledger* (Newark, N.J.), November 17, 1991, pp. 13–14.

Whitlow, Joan. "Strict Monitoring Can Control Diabetes Damage." *The Star-Ledger* (Newark, N.J.), June 20, 1993, p. 6:3.

Internet Addresses

Diseases affect people around the world. Information on these diseases and their effects on people is readily available on the World Wide Web. Major government agencies, health organizations, and medical facilities make a great deal of information on diseases available on their web sites. This information is typically very up-to-date, relatively easy to locate, and available without a trip to a library.

One problem in finding information on diseases on the web is the number of sites that are available. Since there are now over one billion sites on the web, it is increasingly difficult to identify reputable and appropriate sites which meet your informational needs. While you can use a search engine to retrieve some useful sites, such a search may also overwhelm you with thousands of possibilities, many of which may be inaccurate, dated, or inappropriate for your level of interest. This chapter identifies and describes some of the best, most reputable, and stable sites on the web which you can use to find additional information about diabetes.

Internet Addresses researched by: Greg Byerly and Carolyn S. Brodie are Associate Professors in the School of Library and Information Science, Kent State University and write a monthly Internet column titled COMPUTER CACHE for *School Library Media Activities Monthly*.

Web Sites with Information on Diabetes

AIDA On-line
http://www.shodor.org/aida/
Features a "virtual diabetes patient" that allows you to see the changes that insulin and diet have on blood glucose levels. Forty different case scenarios can be simulated to determine the impact of different insulin dosages. Intended for use as an educational and self-learning tool.

American Diabetes Association
http://www.diabetes.org/default.asp
This is the official site of the national organization devoted "to preventing and curing diabetes and to improving the lives of people affected by diabetes" and it provides information about educational services, funding support for research, and patient advocacy. There are articles on current practices in treatment, breakthrough medical advances and health care information for diabetes patients. Features a list of diabetes links.

American Dietetic Association (ADA)
http://www.eatright.org/
The American Dietetic Association (ADA) is the professional organization for dietetic professionals. Provides links to nutrition and health resources through news information, legislative releases and selected links. Search the site for materials on tuberculosis and diet.

Ask NOAH about Diabetes (New York Online Access to Health)
http://www.noah.cuny.edu/diabetes/diabetes.html
Medical librarians from the New York Public Library, the New York Academy of

Medicine and other medical institutions created the New York Online Access to Health (NOAH) to provide access to selected web sites on various diseases and health-related issues. Use this site on diabetes to identify over fifty carefully selected sites on what diabetes is, care and treatment, complications and concerns, and diabetes resources.

Brain Pop: Blood Glucose Movie
http://www.brainpop.com/health/diseases/bloodglucose/index.asp
Brain Pop: Diabetes Movie
http://www.brainpop.com/health/diseases/diabetes/index.asp
These animated cartoons show how you blood sugar levels are monitored through a glucose test for individuals with diabetes and provide basic information about diabetes and treatment.

CDC Diabetes and Public Health Resource
http://www.cdc.gov/diabetes/
This is a public health information site from the Centers for Disease Control and Prevention (CDC) for the sixteen million Americans diagnosed with diabetes. The section on diabetes FAQs is especially helpful in providing information on the symptoms, treatment and prevention of the disease.

Children with Diabetes
http://www.childrenwithdiabetes.com/index_cwd.htm
This site is a comprehensive online resource which provides weekly updated information for children with diabetes and their families. News headlines provide trends in treatment of the disease, a diabetes dictionary defines related terms, and the positive story of a child with diabetes is regularly featured.

Diabetes Digest
http://www.diabetesdigest.com/
This is the web site companion to Diabetes Digest, a print magazine that is distributed through 15,000 pharmacies nationwide. It features diabetes nutrition information, including recipes, current trends in medication, and information on diabetes symptoms and treatments. Basic facts about the disease are briefly outlined.

Diabetes Education and Research Center
http://www.libertynet.org/diabetes/
Check out the FAQs and tips for managing your diabetes to find some very practical information about diabetes. This nonprofit organization also includes news stories about diabetes and links to other good diabetes-related sites.

Diabetes Facts and Figures
http://www.diabetes.org/ada/facts.asp
From the American Diabetes Association, this site provides a good overview of diabetes, including national statistics. Check out: diabetes in youth, diabetes among African Americans, Latinos and Native Americans, diabetes and eye and kidney complications, and profiles of the diagnosed.

Diabetesline
http://www.diabetesline.com/HIST/HIST01.shtm
This site provides easy-to-navigate information on diabetes with sections on diabetes through the ages, diabetes and long-term complications, and nutrition and

diabetes. Good information is also provided on causes, symptoms, and treatment of diabetes.

Discovery of Insulin.com
http://www.discoveryofinsulin.com/
This web site was created to chronicle the historical discovery of insulin in 1921. The site features the life and work of famous researchers including F. G. Banting and J. J. R. MacLeod, both of whom were awarded the 1923 Nobel Prize for Medicine for their work on insulin.

Insulin-Free World Foundation
http://www.insulinfree.org/
This site includes a great deal of practical information on living with diabetes. Sections include: facts and statistics, working to prevent diabetes, pancreas transplants, islet cell replacement, immunology, and mechanical solutions.

Joslin Diabetes Foundation
http://www.joslin.harvard.edu/
From Harvard Medical School, this site provides a wealth of information about diabetes. The sections on research information and education center are especially useful. Individuals with diabetes would also be very interested in the managing diabetes and diabetes news sections.

Juvenile Diabetes Foundation (JDF)
http://www.jdf.org/
This site is produced by one of the most important organization for parents with children diagnosed with diabetes. The goal of the Juvenile Diabetes Foundation (JDF) is "to find a cure for diabetes and its complications through the support of research." The site provides general facts about the disease, advocacy and fund raising support for research, and related current news stories.

Kids Learn About Diabetes
http://www.geocities.com/HotSprings/6935/what_is.html
A very informative and interesting tutorial designed for kids that includes a page of information about diabetes and then a multiple-choice question. After answering the question correctly, you can continue to the next part of the tutorial. Featured parts of the tutorial include: general information about diabetes, insulin, blood and urine testing, balancing insulin, exercise and diet, fears and feelings, and cure and treatment.

National Institute of Diabetes and Digestive and Kidney Diseases: Diabetes Overview
http://www.niddk.nih.gov/health/diabetes/pubs/dmover/dmover. htm#what
Provided by the National Institute of Diabetes and Digestive and Kidney Diseases, one of the National Institutes of Health, this site provides answers to a variety of questions on diabetes, including: "What is Diabetes?" and "What is the Status of Diabetes Research?"

General Medical and Disease Web Sites

AMA Health Insights
http://www.ama-assn.org/consumer.htm
Produced by the American Medical Association, this site offers succinct and

understandable explanations of specific medical conditions and diseases, including hepatitis, the common cold, diabetes, and tuberculosis. This is also a good source for general health and nutrition information.

Centers for Disease Control and Prevention (CDC)
http://www.cdc.gov/
The Centers for Disease Control and Prevention (CDC) is an agency of the Department of Health and Human Services and is comprised of eleven different centers. Consult the Health Topics A to Z to find information on virtually any disease or health topic.

CHID (Combined Health Information Database) ONLINE
http://chid.nih.gov/
CHID is a bibliographic database produced by a wide variety of health-related agencies of the federal government. This is a very comprehensive index of materials and includes many materials not indexed elsewhere.

drkoop.com
http://www.drkoop.com
Offered by Dr. C. Everett Koop, former U.S. Surgeon General, this is a good site for general health and medical information. You can browse through alphabetical listings to find information about specific symptoms or diseases.

Epidemic! The World of Infectious Disease
http://www.amnh.org/exhibitions/epidemic/
Learn all about microbes, how they function, how they can make you sick, and how diseases are spread by visiting this virtual exhibit from the American Museum of Natural History. Be sure to check out the infection, detection, protection section which graphically explains "How Lou Got the Flu" and "Bacteria in the Cafeteria."

Food and Nutrition Information Center
http://www.nal.usda.gov/fnic/etext/fnic.html
Compiled by the Food and Nutrition Information Center of the U.S. Department of Agriculture, this site offers an alphabetical approach to nutrition information. However, you can also go directly to information on dietary supplements, food composition, dietary guidelines, and the food guide pyramid.

Health.gov
http://www.health.gov/
Health.gov is a good place to start when looking for information on diseases and health which has been prepared by various federal agencies.

Infections
http://KidsHealth.org/parent/infections/index.html
This section of the KidsHealth.org site provides information on all sorts of childhood infections. Causes and treatments for over fifty diseases, ranging from flu to mononucleosis, are provided, frequently with drawings or other illustrations. Consult the rest of the KidsHealth.org site for other health-related topics.

Internet FDA (U.S. Food and Drug Administration)
http://www.fda.gov/
As the national consumer protection agency, the FDA regulates and inspects food, cosmetics, medicines, and medical equipment to ensure their safe use. Explore this site for information on biologics, animal and human drugs, children and tobacco, toxicology research, and medical products.

National Institutes of Health
http://www.nih.gov/
The National Institutes of Health (NIH), comprised of 25 separate Institutes and Centers, is one of eight health agencies of the Public Health Service which, in turn, is part of the U.S. Department of Health and Human Services. This site and the sites of the twenty-five Institutes and Centers contain a wealth of health-related materials.

National Library of Medicine
http://www.nlm.nih.gov/
The National Library of Medicine (NLM) is the world's largest medical library. In addition to offering access to MEDLINE and MEDLINEplus, the NLM site includes many other specialized resources, including BioethicsLine, CancerNet, HIV/AIDS facts, and clinical trials.

NetWellness
http://www.netwellness.org/
A great source for consumer health information. Covers health diseases such as influenza, hepatitis, diabetes, mononucleosis, and tuberculosis. Use the search feature to retrieve links to selected web sites and NetWellness articles, reports, and responses to questions submitted to ask an expert.

Office of Rare Diseases
http://rarediseases.info.nih.gov/ord/
Need information on a new or very rare disease? Look no further than the Office of Rare Diseases in the National Institutes of Health for information on diseases ranging from Aarskog Syndrome to Xeroderma Pigmetosum.

U.S. Department of Health and Human Services
http://www.os.dhhs.gov/
This is the home page of the U.S. Department of Health and Human Services. Use the search capability to find information on specific diseases and health problems. Consumer health information is available from the Healthfinder® section of the site.

Virtual Office of the Surgeon General
http://www.surgeongeneral.gov/
Learn about the Office of the Surgeon General and what he does. Check out "What Can You Do" to discover how to "improve your own health, the health of your loved ones, and the health of your community."

World Health Organization
http://www.who.int/
Get an international perspective on health and disease-related issues by consulting this site. Good source of statistics about diseases and health problems around the world.

Index

oral hypoglycemic drugs, 6, 20, 52, 54, 68–69
oral insulin, 88, 98
oral tolerance, 88
Orinase, 68

P

pancreas, 5, 12, 13, 16, 26–28, 29, 42, 50, 63, 101
Paolo, Tony, 34, 51
Paracelsus, 11
photopheresis, 91
Pi-Sunyer, Xavier, 70
Polopolus, Peggy, *86*
pork insulin, 21, 63
prediabetes, 35
predisposition, 41
pregnancy, 35–36, *75, 76*
prevention, 84–92
previous abnormality of glucose tolerance (PrevAGT), 35

R

rat insulin, 21
receptors, 38, 47
recombinant DNA, 21
recombinant human insulin, 21
renal threshold, 30
Robinson, Jackie, 31, *32*, 33
Rollo, John, 12
Rosenthal, Elisabeth, 82
Rosenthal, Robert D., 96

S

Sanger, Frederick, 20
self-monitoring glucose levels, 71–72
Sherwin, Robert, 83
smoking, 80–81
somatostatin, 38
Soon-Shiong, Patrick, 103
stem cells, 102
sugar, 8, 11, 12, 23, 25, 26, 27, 67, 96
sugar metabolism, 27, 37
sugar substitutes, 58–59

sulfonylureas, 20, 68
Susruta, 11
symptoms, 5, 6, 10, 11, 22, 24, 34, 35, 39, 49
synthetic insulin, 20–21

T

Tamborlane, William, 83
target cells, 96
teens, 7, 39–40, 51, 82–83, 84, *86*
testing of blood sugar level, 51, 55, 70, 85
thirst, 10, 11, 23, 34
Thompson, Leonard, 16
thymus gland, 90, 102
tolbutamide, 68
tolrestat, 100
transplants, 101–105
travel, 79
treatment, *19*, 20, 22, 52, 68
treatments, early, 10, 12, 16, 18
Type I diabetes, 5, 9, 22–33, 34, 52, 54, 59, 85–91
Type II diabetes, 6, 9, 18, 20, 24, 34–38, 46, 52, 59, 68, 91–92, 95, 100

U

urination, excessive, 10, 23, 34
urine, sugar in, 9, 11, 12, 23, 30
urine tests, 49, 72

V

vanadium, 105–107
viruses, 42–45
vitamin, B-3 87
von Mering, Joseph, 12

W

Weiner, Howard, 88
White, Priscilla, 41
Wilson, George, 97
work, 76–79
World Health Organization, 69
Wright, James R., Jr., 104